D1592365

THE
RIPPLE
EFFECT

Todd Freiwald
With Shawn McQuaid

Evergreen
PRESS

The lessons contained in this book are intended to lay a basic foundation for learning wilderness skills. They are intended to be informative and fun. To that end, caution for the safety of all involved should be exercised at all times. Wilderness food items should not be consumed unless the reader can positively identify them and is absolutely sure they are safe to ingest. Water should never be consumed unless the reader is sure it has been purified and is safe to drink. Fire making skills should only be practiced where permissible and if the reader is in a safe, well-ventilated area—ensuring that they have the ability to control, monitor, and extinguish the fire. We encourage readers to have a plan, be prepared for emergencies, and always exercise common sense. Since this is not a comprehensive treatise on any of these aspects of survival skills, neither the author nor the publisher will be held liable for injuries or damages resulting from using these instructions.

The Ripple Effect
by Todd Freiwald
Copyright ©2010 Todd Freiwald

ISBN 978-1-58169-345-4
For Worldwide Distribution
Printed in the U.S.A.

Evergreen Press
P.O. Box 191540 • Mobile, AL 36619
800-367-8203

Table of Contents

Dedication
To my wonderful wife, Wendy—
on rainy days you patiently stood by as I made fire in our garage.
You always gave more than you ever took. Without your love
and support, the ministry and this book
would not have been possible.

To Jake, Ryan, Scott, Megan, Cole, and Erin—
may the example we set be
pleasing to God.

"As iron sharpens iron, so one man sharpens another"
(Proverbs 27:17).

Special Thanks
Col. Wayne Sinclair, USMC. My brother Rat, my brother in arms
and my brother in Christ—your friendship, guidance,
and support continue to be invaluable.

Holly Cooley —for donating her time and artistic talent to this book. A
picture is truly worth a thousand words

LtCol. Fred Gross, Jr. USA (Ret.)

Dr. Clark King, USMC (Ret.)

Banks Swanson
Pastor, Shenandoah Community Fellowship Church

Ron Croom

Anthony Neri, M.D.

Jerry Lopes

United States Marine Corps Mountain Warfare Training Center
Bridgeport, California

Prologue

I looked for a man among them who would build up the wall and stand before me in the gap on behalf of the land so I would not have to destroy it, but I found none (Ezekiel 22:30).

The world can be a very dangerous place. Is your son ready? Nowadays, much discussion is heard about raising sons. I fully understand the good intentions implied when the term raising is used, but the word does not adequately describe our deeper responsibility as earthly fathers in God's kingdom. You raise cows; you train sons. Give a calf what it wants and you will soon have a cow—ripe for slaughter. Training implies something far deeper.

Training is deliberate, purposeful, and has a specific objective to be achieved; it is not by chance or mere coincidence. As a father, you alone are ordained by God with the responsibility for the training and biblical education of your son. *You may delegate that authority to someone else, but you may never delegate your responsibility.* If you do not train your son according to God's will and purpose, then the world will train your son according to its will and purpose. Whom do you trust? God is looking for men to build a wall and stand before Him, and God makes it perfectly clear that it is your responsibility to train those men.

The Bible makes many references to the wilderness; God

used it to forge a nation, to deliver the message of the coming Messiah, and to test His Son. So it was to the wilderness that my friend Shawn and I wanted to take our sons—to train them and, as it turned out, to be trained. The wilderness is the perfect laboratory for this world; if you can learn how survive in it, you can survive anywhere.

With that revelation, Shawn and I began our first deliberate steps into the wild with our sons. We always loved the wilderness, but now it took on new meaning as we had a purpose for being there. We started small—on a cold, rainy day five years ago—and gradually, prayerfully gained focus until a lay ministry was formed. It was not a ministry of two mere men, rather a ministry of fathers united in one purpose—to train up their sons in the way they should go and to give their sons the training, tools, and skill to survive in an ungodly world. We hope you will join us.

Chapter One

The Ripple Effect

"I am about to go the way of all the earth," he said. "So be strong, show yourself a man, and observe what the Lord your God requires" (1 Kings 2:2-3).

When my family moved to Virginia, one of the first people I met was a sheriff's deputy named Bruce. He was described by many of those who knew him as "nuts." He is an old school law man who had his fair share of vehicle pursuits, gun fights, and near death experiences. Crazy or not, he was said to be an avid hunter and trapper who knew the local area like the back of his hand. I was told that he had the ability to bag those monster bucks as easily as my wife could load her shopping cart for a family of six. As a hunter myself, I wanted to talk to this guy!

The majority of my hunting memories revolve around frozen toes and not much else. As I got to know Bruce, I noticed that he seemed to keep his distance from people—always watching, listening, observing. He didn't do this in an arrogant or sinister way; he was just taking in his surroundings. Over the course of a year, I realized two things about Bruce. First, Bruce is not nuts; he is brilliant. Second, Bruce has an understanding of God and His creation that is as deep and profound as anyone I have ever met.

One time Bruce and I were talking about hunting that big, elusive white tail buck—the one many hunters claimed to have seen but few seem to get. I asked Bruce about hunting strategies because I have been to Bruce's house and observed hundreds of antlers, both discarded and mounted, any one of which would make even the most experienced hunter stand in quiet admiration. Bruce explained to me how he moved into and through the forest. Bruce uses no scent block or special soap to mask his odor in the woods or expensive gizmos to track the animals, and wears no fancy clothing. He uses observation, wisdom, and patience.

On several occasions I've had the fortune of walking in the forest with Bruce. At first I felt like a blind man whose eyes were just opened. As Bruce and I moved deeper into the mountains, I was amazed; nothing seemed to escape his attention. From the terrain and how it affected wind patterns to the trees with occasional nibbles on leaves, he noticed every pertinent detail. More than just an observer, Bruce interprets what he sees to paint a picture in his mind from which he can see the rhythms and movements of the forest. Similar to looking at the inner workings of a ticking clock— from the smallest creature to the largest—Bruce understands how they interact, how they live, and how they survive.

This is the kind of knowledge that enables Bruce to coax a fox to step on the two inch pressure pad of a trap in the middle of a field or to nail a twelve point buck in locations that other hunters claimed were utterly devoid of deer. Bruce explained his presence in the wilderness in terms of a "ripple effect." He described his first steps into the forest as being like dropping a pebble into a pond—waves are sent forth in all directions.

As Bruce described it, a chipmunk spends its entire life in an area covering about forty square yards. If you enter his little world, he will know it and will have something to say about it. A squirrel living outside the chipmunk's range does not understand the language of the chipmunk, but it does know when the chipmunk is upset by something. The squirrel will sound an alarm to his friends that something is amiss; something is coming. The deer browsing 100 yards away from the squirrel does not "speak squirrel," but it does know when a squirrel is upset; and so the deer is now alert. Bruce explained that by simply finding ways to limit his negative ripple effect in the wilderness, his chances of success as a hunter were vastly increased.

This approach had me thinking about other ripple effects in life, such as my own effect on the world around me. What message is being transmitted about my presence at any given location or time? Am I a living example of Christ-like behavior? How do my actions affect my children; what legacy will I leave them?

I tell you the truth, the Son can do nothing by himself; he can do only what he sees his Father doing, because whatever the Father does the Son also does (John 5:19).

One day I saw an Associated Press[1] article in my local paper on U.S. Army recruiting. Essentially, the article explained the incentives the Army is using to attract prospective enlistees in its target age group of seventeen to twenty-four year olds. The real story, I believe, was in the graph that accompanied the article. According to the Army, only 15 percent of seventeen- to twenty-four-year-old (youth) males in the United States are qualified and available to serve in the military. Another 11 percent of youth are eligible but enrolled in higher education. The shocker is that 17 percent of America's youth are simply disqualified from national military service due to drug or alcohol abuse.

Just as troubling, a group comprising 9 percent of our nation's young men are ineligible due to criminal convictions. Now, if you have ever been to a military recruiter, you know that a certain amount of drug and alcohol experimentation can be waived for an applicant who is otherwise highly qualified. Similarly, the Army can waive certain criminal convictions if the candidate is exceptionally qualified. Yes, the numbers are a bit skewed but not in a favorable way. The bottom line is that although 26 percent of our youth can serve our nation, an equal number cannot serve because of drug abuse, alcohol abuse, or criminal activity. The numbers of drug and alcohol abusers and criminals are probably greater, but some have yet to either admit to it or be caught.

The remaining 48 percent were not eligible to serve for a variety of factors including too many dependents, failure to pass mental aptitude examinations, physical limitations or conditions, or emotional handicaps. These numbers are alarming by any measure. On the surface, one might conclude that American parents can expect that more than a quarter of their sons will become involved in crime, drugs, and alcohol abuse to such a degree as to make them unqualified to wear their country's uniform.

These statistics are not by chance. We are in the midst of a spiritual war, and the stakes could not be higher. The battle is for the hearts and minds of our sons. We can and must win, but our victory will require purposeful training. The ripple effect with your son begins in your home.

Fathers, do not exasperate your children; instead, bring them up in the training and instruction of the Lord (Ephesians 6:4).

The purpose of this book is to provide fathers, either individually or in groups, with a practical means to prepare and equip their sons not only to survive as young men but also to create a godly ripple throughout their journeys in this wilderness we call life. Only one man in this world was ordained by God to train your son, and that is you. You alone carry the responsibility for your son's training. We all have dreams for our children, and if we think about it, we probably could articulate the kind of man we want our sons to become.

I have never met a man that wanted his son to grow up to be insecure, an adulterer, an alcoholic, abusive to his spouse or children, cowardly, weak, or timid. We can sit around and hope that our sons grow to be men of integrity and character. While we can have the best intentions in the world, I am reminded by what a U.S. Marine Corps friend of mine once said to me, "Hope is not a course of action. Only with thorough planning and preparation can you expect to accomplish your objectives."

In other words, hope and intentions by themselves are not enough. You must prayerfully, purposefully, and deliberately pursue your goals. Those who have coached a sports team know the value of practice; no team can expect to win without it. As any coach worthy of the title will tell you, champions are made during the off season. If you wait until the season begins before conditioning and practicing, you may as well stay home.

> *Dividing up his cloths, they cast lots to see what each would get* (Mark 15:24).

When we die, each of us will stand before the throne of God and give an accounting of our lives. All of our worldly spoils will be divided up and taken by those we leave behind. I cringe when I read how when Jesus hung on the cross, suffering for my sins, men stood around and cast lots for His clothing. Will our sons simply gamble for our possessions? Will we leave only that which robbers can steal, and moths and rust destroy? Or will our mission be to train and educate our sons to be godly men grounded in faith, secure in their surroundings, and know they have been left with the greatest gift of all—the kingdom of heaven?

> *So David triumphed over the Philistine with a sling and a stone* (1 Samuel 17:50).

One day our sons will have to stand and face their "Goliath." All of us have fought giants of our own—either temptation, lust, guilt, shame, or some major upset or failure in life. Our sons will face a Goliath, and they will have a choice—stand firm with their faith in God or flee and hide. Will they be ready?

This book provides a simple way for fathers to begin a

positive ripple in the world by training their sons to survive in the literal wilderness as a means to prepare for the figurative wilderness that is the world in which we live. Basic wilderness survival training is linked to biblical principles. Together, these will equip you to train your son with the knowledge, skills, and confidence to survive in the wilderness, and more importantly the world. The book is not intended to be the definitive word on wilderness survival or Christian training. Rather, it is intended to be a step in a journey that fathers and sons can take together toward the ultimate goal of authentic Christian manhood.

We chose to use the four basic elements of wilderness survival as object lessons to train our sons to survive in an ungodly world. Each element corresponds to the four pillars of Christian living.

Shelter represents *Christian fellowship*
Water represents *Prayer*
Food represents the *Word of God*
Fire represents a *Servant Heart*

If you can account for the four physical elements, you can survive anywhere in the world. Likewise, if you can account for the four spiritual elements, you can survive anything this ungodly world will throw at you. Why did we choose the wilderness as our classroom? The reason is simple. Where did the Spirit lead Jesus before He could begin His ministry on earth? The wilderness . . .

Chapter 2

Survival Mindset

Finally, be strong in the Lord and in his mighty power.
Put on the full armor of God so that you can take your
stand against the devil's schemes (Ephesians 6:10-11).

Recently my family travelled to the Outer Banks off the coast of North Carolina with some other families during the peak of the beach vacation season. My ten-year-old son, Scott, was playing in the ocean with his brothers, his sister, Megan, and some other kids about thirty yards north of our umbrella. The day was beautiful and sunny; the beach crowded to capacity. The large numbers of beach goers concerned my wife, Wendy, and me. Wendy wanted to go for a walk on the beach with her friend and asked me to have the kids move closer to us so I could keep a better eye on them.

I sent word to the kids, and gradually they worked themselves closer. After about twenty minutes, I realized Scott was missing; I was mildly concerned. In God I trust, but after seventeen years in law enforcement, everyone else needs to keep their hands where I can see them. I conducted the routine interviews of the other kids who unanimously replied, "I don't know where he is." I gathered the kids and organized a search. We couldn't find him.

I began to feel mild panic. I thought, *Keep calm and don't make assumptions. Wendy is gone; we'll find Scott soon.* Our friends and all the kids organized a bigger search—some to the beach house and others went 400 yards north and south of our location to no avail. Mild panic turned to fear. My prayers became more intense.

Other families joined in the effort, and concern was written on everyone's face. Could the culprit be a riptide or an abductor? I found myself torn between gut-wrenching fear and anger . . . *What would I say to Wendy when she returned?* Between searching and praying, over an hour had passed since Scott was last seen. I finally went to the beach patrol for assistance.

Thank God, the beach patrol found Scott within five minutes! He was fine. I heard the call over the radio just as Wendy walked up to me. Her face said it all. I cannot tell you how thankful I was to be able to look at her and say, "They found him; he is fine." They found Scott two miles south of us—walking, searching, and hoping to see Mom or Dad. Driving Scott back to us on those crowded shores took the beach patrol several minutes.

As I waited with Wendy, I chatted with one of the beach patrol officers. Interestingly, he said that they conduct several such "rescues" every week. The captain said that children under ten will almost always pick the direction they think is correct and keep going. The beach patrol brought Scott back, and the experience still brings a tear to my eye. I think about all the different ways the situation could have turned out had Scott not been rescued.

Scott did the best he could with what he knew. As I thought about it, I knew his predicament had been my fault. I realized that I had been more concerned about sunscreen and boogie boards than helping my son by pointing out landmarks and giving him the necessary knowledge and skills so if he did become disoriented, lost, or confused, he could find his way to safety.

I am sending you out like sheep among wolves. Therefore be as shrewd as snakes and as innocent as doves (Matthew 10:16).

Dangers need to be considered when journeying through the wilderness. The temperature extremes, dehydration, starvation, and disorientation can all mean death for the man who is untrained to overcome these challenges. The overwhelming majority of wilderness accidents occur with what is referred to as the day hiker mentality. Simply put, a day hiker mentality means being unprepared for the unexpected and lacking even the most basic survival skills and equipment.

Likewise, the spiritual day hiker is also untrained, unprepared, and prone to fall into the snares of temptation and disobedience. As Christians, we have been chosen as a sworn enemy of Satan. While our salvation is secured through the blood of Jesus, we are in a constant spiritual battle. Satan has us in his cross hairs, and he will probe us, always seeking a vulnerable place to attack when we least expect it. Our successes and victories against Satan's schemes will hinge on our level of spiritual training and preparedness. Survival, whether physical or spiritual, requires four basic elements:

Food — the Word of God
Water — Prayer
Fire — A Servant's Heart
Shelter — Fellowship

If we can account for these four physical elements, we can survive anywhere in the world. Likewise, if we can account for the four spiritual elements, we can endure anything Satan would throw at us. Life will present challenges that test our faith or threaten our lives. Whether we are lost in the wilderness or dealing with some moral crisis at work or home, how we respond says a great deal about our preparedness and training.

Have you ever played that game with a friend where you put out your hands, palms up, and your friend lays his hands on yours, palm to palm, and you try to slap the backs of his hands before he can pull them away? If you have, then you know the principle that action is faster than reaction. Life is full of adversity, and those who can respond correctly enough and quickly enough are more likely to succeed and survive. This is one of the reasons the military and law enforcement are big on acronyms. They make things easier and quicker to remember. For example, a commonly used acronym is KISS for Keep It Simple, Stupid.

In dealing with crises, I wanted to create a survival acronym that every young man could easily remember and use to help guide him. I also wanted to apply the KISS principle to it. Above all, I wanted to teach young men to be godly men of action. How can I teach young men to see situations through God's eyes, act within God's will, and be mentally prepared for and know how to respond when a crisis strikes? I wanted an acronym that could be applied to any situation in life at any time. The answer was "PEE-PEE."

PEE-PEE
P – Pray
E – Evaluate
E – Equipment
P – Plan
E – Expect
E - Execute

Be joyful always; pray continually; give thanks in all cir-cumstances, for this is God's will for you in Christ Jesus (1 Thessalonians 5:16-17).

PRAY: In any situation, our very first action should be to seek the wisdom, guidance, and comfort of the Lord. Talk to God and allow Him to clear your mind of shock, uncertainty, and fear. Whether you are lost in the woods, faced with a tough decision at school, or simply waking up to begin a new day, you should turn to the Lord and pray for His guidance and counsel.

Praying should be the first active step you take before making any decision. Talking to God prepares the mind and fortifies the spirit. Prayer helps us bring a situation into focus from a more godly perspective. If you make decisions when you are afraid or angry, the resulting actions will be tainted by those emotions. Additionally, if you make decisions without talking to God, you risk acting outside of His will. Either way, the result may not be good. Pray.

The mocker seeks wisdom and finds none, but knowledge comes easily to the discerning (Proverbs 14:6).

EVALUATE: Observe, observe, observe. The military would call this *situational awareness.* You may not know ex-actly where you are or how you got there, but God gave you eyes, ears, a nose, and a brain. Stop, look, and listen. Do you see power lines, a trail or road, or a radio antenna? Listen for voices, cars, planes, farm or domestic animals, or any sound that is not native to the wilderness. What time of year is it; what time of day is it? Are you high up on a mountain or down in a valley? What is the weather, the terrain?

Are there drugs or alcohol at the party? Is your new friend a Christian? Is that movie or music appropriate? All of these observations mean something, and how correctly you interpret their meanings can keep you from harm.

Finally, be strong in the Lord and in his mighty power. Put on the full armor of God so that you can take your stand against the devil's schemes (Ephesians 6:10-11).

EQUIPMENT: Inventory your resources. Lay out every piece of equipment you posses, right down to your underwear, and study it. Resources may be matches, your Bible, a shoelace, a stream, a sleeping bag, a blackberry bush, or a Christian friend. Take a moment and ask yourself, *Based on what I have, what are my options and capabilities; and what are my shortcomings?* In a survival situation, everything you have must be evaluated for its usefulness. Having the equipment or training to account for only three out of four elements of survival (Food/the Word; Water/Prayer; Fire/Service; Shelter/Fellowship) can leave you just as bad off as if you had none at all. It all counts, and the usefulness of your resources will be solely dependant on your level of practice and skill.

Every prudent man acts out of knowledge, but a fool exposes his folly (Proverbs 13:16).

PLAN: By now you have talked to God and can make rational decisions. You have a general feel for the environment you are in, and you have made an inventory of available resources. You know the four elements of survival are Food/the Word, Water/Prayer, Fire/Service, and Shelter/Fellowship.

First, prioritize your tasks based on your evaluation of your environmental conditions. For example, if it's a clear January day, perhaps you should build a fire before working on a shelter. Conversely, if it's raining, you should consider building a shelter first that will provide a dry place to begin your fire. Second, prioritize your tasks based on your resources or lack thereof. Finally, you must prioritize your tasks based on reasonable assumptions. For example, in a hot climate it is reasonable to assume that you will require additional water.

> *As you know, we consider blessed those who have persevered. You have heard of Job's perseverance and have seen what the Lord finally brought about. The Lord is full of compassion and mercy* (James 5:11).

EXPECT: Much of the preparation is mental, and being preconditioned as to what challenges might be faced can go a long way toward your ability to survive adversity. Expect that you will be lost, cold, wet, and hungry for a few days. Know that God is with you. Being mentally prepared to face challenges is critical, and that mental preparation comes from practice. Your ability to overcome adversity is directly proportional to the training and practice you have before that adversity strikes. Once adversity comes, you can face it in one of two ways: actively (focusing on solutions) or passively (focusing on the problem).

Expecting that they will have to endure hardship can be a difficult concept to teach young men, but it is important. The way that we can effectively do this is to teach them to be actively busy, focusing on their planned priorities.

A little sleep, a little slumber, a little folding of the hands to rest–and poverty will come on you like a bandit and scarcity like an armed man (Proverbs 6:10-11).

EXECUTE: Be actively busy. A shelter can be built or improved, wood can be gathered, food and water found, and a fire started. Prayers can be offered, and Scripture can be read. The more you think about what you can be doing, the less you will focus on how bad your situation is. Many military leaders have written about the importance of keeping the troops busy in times of war and peace. If they have too much downtime, troops will find things to keep themselves busy—not always the right things.

Fear, apprehension, doubt, mischief, and all the negative thoughts that Satan brings to the table will be spread out before you to ponder. Get busy, stay busy, and pray without ceasing.

For God did not give us a spirit of timidity, but a spirit of power, of love and of self-discipline (2 Timothy 1:7).

The goal of a survival mindset is to mentally prepare young men for the unforeseen and unexpected challenges—the Goliaths—that will inevitably face them in life. It is our duty as fathers to introduce our sons to their heavenly Father and to give them a solid biblical education. We must also provide them with the tools they will need to maneuver through the pitfalls of this world. We will never be able to teach our sons how to deal with each and every possible situation, danger, or temptation. But we can lay a solid foundation that will give them the peace and confidence that comes only to those who rest in Jesus Christ.

Chapter 3

Fire: A Servant's Heart

Be dressed ready for service and keep your lamps burning
(Luke 12:35).

Roy Marshall is one of those uniquely gifted men we encounter from time to time who is not easily forgotten. He has
a confident, reassuring presence about him—a sort of "man's
man" who is seldom without a smile on his face, a fire in his
eyes, or the Bible in his hand.

Roy's life has one purpose: to live for Christ. Roy owns
The Gym, a donations-only power lifting gym in the small
town of Woodstock, Virginia, where he trains young men and
women in the mental and physical discipline of weight
training.

Roy's gym serves two purposes. First, his primary plat-
form is to speak the gospel in love and truth; and second, the
donations he collects for the gym also go to support a food
mission called The Lighthouse Grocery, which helps to feed
the hungry and homeless in Woodstock.

During one of our father/son ministry campouts, I asked
Roy if he would be willing to talk to the men and their boys
in an informal setting. Roy agreed and delivered a captivating
sermon for about an hour around the crackling campfire. The
topic of his sermon was courage and sacrifice. I remember
well the three examples Roy gave in the form of questions
and answers:

1. Who is the most feared soldier on the battlefield?
The soldier who already considers himself dead.

2. Who is the most feared fighter in the ring?
The fighter who can ignore pain.

3. Who is the most feared runner on the track?
The runner who refuses to quit.

Roy's life is dedicated to living according to what Paul said in Romans 12:1, to be "living sacrifices, holy and pleasing to God." Roy is a living example of the soldier, the fighter, and the runner. Roy's passion for service burns like a flame. Few who come into contact with him can deny that his warmth and brilliance is not palpable—like the campfire he stood beside when he delivered his sermon that cold morning.

Fire

Fire is one of the most basic of all survival needs. Fire provides warmth, light, comfort, security, and hope. It can cook your food, boil and purify water, signal for help, or light the way. Making fire requires as much art as it does science, and your understanding of the science coupled with your practice of the art will be what can mean the difference between living and dying.

To understand the science of fire you need to understand the fire triangle: fire needs oxygen, heat, and fuel to exist. If any one of these three is missing, fire is impossible.

We have different gifts, according to the grace given us (Romans 12:6).

Serving others means having an outward focus on the needs of others rather than dwelling on your own problems. This outward focus reminds you of your blessings and keeps you spiritually vibrant. Just as fire provides many benefits, your service to others acts as a fire that offers hope, warmth, comfort, and light.

To understand the science of service, you need to understand the service triangle: time, talent, and treasure. Countless ways and opportunities are possible and available to serve both large and small. However, unlike the fire triangle, the service triangle is not interdependent: you do not need to employ all three to be a good servant. The art of service is in understanding how you can best serve the needs of the church and those around you with the time, talent, or treasure that God provides.

TIME: Everyone has 24 hours in a day, but for many this element is the most challenging to apply. A thousand things constantly seem to compete for a precious few hours. Pray for guidance in prioritizing responsibilities and commitments as well as the discernment to make time each week to provide some useful service to others that glorifies God.

TALENT: God has blessed each of you with talents. Some Christians have not yet discovered all their gifts, much less realized how God can use them. You can often identify your talents or gifts by following your passion or concerns for the needs of others. Sometimes you may need to remember that these gifts were given for the glory of God. Ask God to find ways to use these in the service of others.

TREASURE: Matthew 19:16-22 tells us of a rich young man who asked Jesus what he must do to obtain eternal life. After some discussion about following various commandments, in which the man assures Jesus he has followed all since youth, Jesus instructs him to do what soon becomes apparent is the hardest of all—to sell all of his possessions, give the money to the poor, and follow Him. The rich man's reaction is telling. He went away grieving because he owned much property.

Inwardly people empathize with the young man; selling all his earthly belongings and giving away the proceeds seems a bit harsh. But Jesus' lesson was not that poverty leads to salvation but that material wealth can harden your heart and blind you to the needs of others and your own personal shortcomings. Pray for opportunities and discretion in the use of your material blessings and abundance in such a way as to serve others and light a fire of hope and contentment that glorifies God.

In the wilderness, you build a fire to meet a need. The need can be both physical and psychological. In the world, your service is like a fire that serves to meet others' needs. Additionally, your service to others provides a sense of self-worth as you work to glorify God. To take this analogy to a practical level, an examination of the basics of fire-making can offer insights into godly servitude.

Making Fire

Regardless of what method you choose to make your fire, some basic principles of fire-making apply: location, fuel, organization and ignition.

LOCATION: When choosing where to build your fire, several considerations need to be taken into account in order to maximize the benefits of a fire without undue risk.

- Is it protected from the wind?
- How close is it to your shelter?
- Can you concentrate its heat where it is most needed?
- Do you have an ample supply of fuel?
- Can you contain the flame?

FUEL: For making and sustaining fire, fuel has three categories:
- *Tinder*: dried grass, shredded cedar bark, cotton, lint, old bird's nests, or almost any fine, dry biodegradable material will work adequately.
- *Kindling*: twigs and sticks (the size of a pencil and smaller) and larger pieces of bark.
- *Wood*: Larger pieces of dead wood will best sustain a flame. Dried dung from an herbivore is a suitable substitute.

SURVIVAL NOTE: Smaller fires require less fuel, are easier to control, and allow for more efficient cooking and providing warmth.

ORGANIZATION: In fire-making, preparation is essential to success. Regardless of what method you use to ignite your fire, gather everything required first. Lay all the various materials out in separate piles. Once you think you have enough tinder and kindling, double that amount. Put your three types of fuel into separate piles—close enough to your fire for easy access but far enough away so they won't be an accidental fire hazard.

If the fire is needed for warmth and light to get you through the night, be sure to stage enough wood. Ten pounds of dry fuel for each hour required is a good estimate. After all, no one wants to be searching for wood at 2:00 a.m. when its fifteen degrees outside.

SURVIVAL NOTE: Avoid gathering wood that has been lying on the ground. This wood will absorb ground moisture, may be hard to burn, and may be very smoky. Seek dead, dry branches that are still on trees or off the ground.

IGNITION (the spark): There are many ways to ignite a fire, but the basics of location, fuel, and organization are the same. The following four methods are covered in this book:

1. One match
2. Magnesium and flint
3. Magnifying glass
4. Friction

Serving Others

Just as each of us has one body with many members, and these members do not all have the same function, so in Christ we who are many form one body, and each member belongs to all the others (Romans 12:4-5).

Service is an outward reflection of your love for Jesus Christ and bears good witness to our Father in heaven. Therefore, Christians have a responsibility to match the three elements of service with the needs of the church body and the community where it belongs or can best influence. This is not a daunting task. There are countless opportunities to serve. Whether you meet the need of a single individual or support your church body as a whole, service still matters! Just as a survival fire provides warmth and light that in turn gives us hope, so too does service to the glory of God give others warmth, light, and more importantly, hope.

> *Then I heard the voice of the Lord saying, "Whom shall I send? And who will go for us?" And I said, "Here am I. Send me!"* (Isaiah 6:8).

LOCATION: Identifying good places to serve begins with prayer. Ask God to use you where needs exist. Look for opportunities highlighted in church bulletins, talk to church leaders, and pray for God's leading. Here are some basic questions to help you get started.
- What are your gifts and talents?
- What needs do you know about in your community or church?
- Can you meet that need by yourself or can you enlist the help of others?

> *Just as the Son of Man did not come to be served, but to serve* (Matthew 20:28).

FUEL: Regardless of how you choose to serve, it will require part or the entire service triangle (time, talent, and treasure). Here are some examples of different ways to be a servant.
- Rick, a retired executive, agreed to sponsor a boy in the father/son ministry. Each gathering, Rick picks the boy up

and trains with him in the wilderness. He is a positive male role model for a boy who has no father figure in his life.

• The new addition at a church required a lot of electrical work. A church member, a retired electrician, donated both his time and talent to insure that the building project would be completed on time and under budget.

• Recently a church sought to install a $2,500 power-point system to display the words to the music on a screen. A call went out to the congregation, and before the service was over someone anonymously donated $1000 toward the system.

Who then is the faithful and wise manager, whom the master puts in charge of his servants to give them their food allowance at the proper time? (Luke 12:42).

ORGANIZATION: The goal of being a good servant is to glorify our Father in heaven. To that end you must prepare and apportion the gifts God has given you so they can be used to their best result. Remember, hope is not a course of action. Here are some questions you should consider:

• Is the project clearly defined?
• Are the required elements from the service triangle available?

Pray about and think through what you wish to do, and be sure you give your best effort since your service is a reflection of your love for God. If you have any questions, ask your church leaders for advice.

Practice Your Survival Skills

As with any survival skill, we strongly recommend that you practice the skills and techniques before you need them. Although fire is an essential survival tool, it can also be highly destructive and dangerous.

Before practicing fire-making skills, be sure you are in a safe, well-ventilated area and can control the fire. Make sure you have adequate means to put the fire out when you're done. God calls us to be good stewards. Have a plan, be prepared for emergencies, and always exercise common sense.

THE ONE MATCH FIRE

Time Required: 1 hour.

Equipment Required: Bible, matches

Find a Location and Get Organized: Choose a good location to build a fire. Prepare your fire bed and gather the three types of fuel.

Ignition: Everyone knows how to light a match. Instant fire . . . Easy, right? Nevertheless, it is worth your time to have your son practice making a fire with only one match. Be patient, focus on the basics, and watch that wind! The first time my son attempted this it took about a dozen matches before we had fire. That is eleven wasted matches had we been in a real survival situation.

Once Your Fire Is Going:
• Memory Verse: Matthew 5:14-16
• Take a moment and study your fire.

Discuss:
• How is service like building a fire for someone else?

- How do our good deeds affect others?
- What are some ways we can let our light shine before men?

MAGNESIUM AND FLINT FIRE

Time Required: 1 hour.

Equipment Required:

- Bible
- Magnesium and flint block
- Knife or steel striker

Find a Location and Get Organized: Choose a good location to build a fire. Prepare your fire bed and gather the three types of fuel.

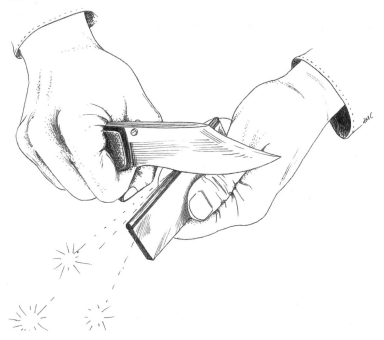

Ignition: Arrange a tinder basket in the shape of a bird's nest. Dry cedar bark works well for this. Take the blade of your knife and carefully shave pieces of magnesium into the basket. Get a good amount of magnesium shavings into the basket. The more shavings you have, the more likely the sparks from the flint will ignite them quickly.

Once you have done this, take your knife blade and drag it forcefully toward the basket in short, brisk movements. The knife should be positioned so the back of blade is pointing toward the basket, and the edge of the blade is pointing toward you. This will focus the sparks toward the magnesium. Use short, powerful strokes and take care not to disrupt the basket with the knife blade or you may have to start all over.

SURVIVAL NOTE: Knives or strikers made from high carbon steel create more sparks on flint than stainless steel blades.

Once Your Fire Is Going:
• Memory Verse: Romans 12:6-8

Discuss:
• What your son believes his gifts and abilities are.
• What spiritual gifts and qualities you see in your son.
• How could he use his gifts and abilities to best serve others?

MAGNIFYING GLASS FIRE

Time Required: 1 hour.
Equipment Required:
• Bible
• Magnifying glass
Find a Location and Get Organized: Choose a good location to build a fire. Prepare your fire bed and gather the three types of fuel.

SURVIVAL NOTE: The key to using a magnifying glass is using the finest tinder you can.

Ignition: Using a magnifying glass to light a fire is common sense. Most of us born before the era of home video games and the Internet spent many summer afternoons trying to burn bugs on the sidewalk with a magnifying glass. Get comfortable and be patient. Ensure you can be in a position to add air (blow) while maintaining the focus of the sunlight.

Once Your Fire Is Going:
Memory Verse: Romans 12:4
Discuss:
• Identify all the ways your son sees people serve in your church.
• Ways people serve he may not have noticed.
• How does each of those acts of service benefit the church as a whole?

THE FRICTION FIRE—Bow/Drill Method

Time Required: 1 hour to numerous attempts.

Equipment Required:
• Bible
• Hearth or fire board
• Bow
• Drill or spindle
• Rope/twine/string
• Drill cap
• Coal catcher
• Fuel

Find a Location and Get Organized: Choose a good location to build a fire. Prepare your fire bed and gather the three types of fuel.

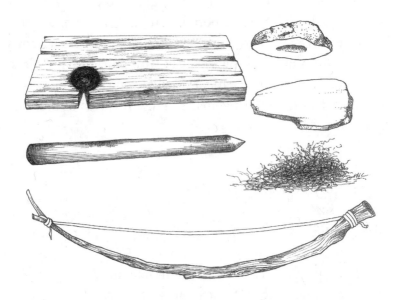

Ignition: Making a friction fire; that is, rubbing sticks together to make a fire is by far the most challenging method in fire-making. There are numerous proven techniques for friction fires. All friction fires require both skill and perseverance but will prove to be the most rewarding in terms of personal achievement.

Keep in mind when making a friction fire, what you are really making is a red hot coal, approximately the size of a pea, that you transfer to your tinder basket to make your fire. It takes practice, effort, and patience to do this. To master this skill may take awhile, but persevere because the reward is great.

When it comes to friction fires, God did not create all wood equally. Not all wood performs well for friction fires. I would recommend researching what local woods works well and are native to your area. Some very good websites offer lots of great information and additional insight on this subject.

Some of the woods that we have researched and work well include but are not limited to: ash, cedar, pine, oak, walnut, cottonwood and sumac (sumac for the drill only). The key to the friction fire is to make sure that your drill and hearth are woods of different density (for example, pine hearth and walnut drill).

SURVIVAL NOTE: Your materials MUST be bone dry to make fire. If your hearth or drill is damp or contains moisture, all your initial efforts (sweat) will be spent "drying" out the wood.

One successful method is using a pine for a hearth and sumac as a drill. This combination works well since sumac has a super soft center, which focuses the heat around the outer portion of the drill. This requires far less effort than using a traditional wood-like cedar.

Making a hearth involves carving a small hole or impression into the hearth about one fourth to one half an inch from the edge of the board just large enough for your drill to fit in. Now, take a pocketknife or some sharp object and carefully cut a section of the hearth out in the shape of a slice of pie with its tip being located in the center of the hole or depression you carved.

Shape the cut out so that the coal dust you generate falls easily onto the coal catcher. The coal catcher can be any dry material capable of temporarily holding a coal: tin foil, leather, heavy cotton or wool fabric, leaf or bark, and should be positioned directly under the hearth socket.

To set in motion a balance between the speed and pressure of your drill, make sure the drill is a straight as possible. Wrap the string from the bow once around the drill, and set it into the socket of the hearth. Again, you may need to adjust the string tension to fit your specific drill. If it is too tight, the drill will keep "jumping" off the hearth. If it is too loose, the drill will not turn.

Survival Note: You will want to lubricate the top portion of your drill by rubbing it next to your nose. The natural oils produced by your face help reduce friction in the drill cap. Do not lubricate the end of the drill that fits into the hearth socket.

Place the cut-out section of your hearth directly over your coal catcher. Wrap the string around your drill one time, and place the drill into the hearth socket. If you are right handed, place your left foot on the hearth to keep it in place; left handed folks need to do the opposite. Place your drill cap over the top (lubricated) end of the drill (to help reduce friction in the drill cap by making its hole larger than the drill). When you begin with the bow, start with smooth, even strokes until you get a rhythm going.

Gradually speed up the pace and increase pressure at the same time. Depending on the wood choice (forty to sixty seconds with a sumac drill and pine hearth), you will begin to see smoke. Now it is really time to get going. Add speed and pressure, and drill as fast as you can until the smoke is very pronounced.

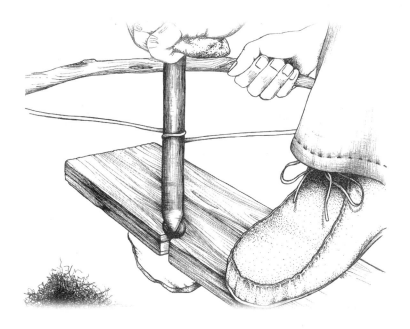

Carefully remove your hearth from on top of your coal catcher. You should see what appears to be a pile of black coal dust that is smoking slightly. The coal dust should appear black and almost feathery. (If the dust is not smoking or is brown, start over.) Blow gently, and you should see an orange glow.

Carefully transfer your "coal" into your tinder basket. Your tinder basket should be about the size of a grapefruit and have a place to hold your coal. Bird's nests work very well for this, or you can shape one out of cedar bark. Place the coal into the tinder basket, and blow gently and constantly until flames appear. As long as you can see an orange glow, DO NOT stop blowing until flames appear. Once flames appear, carefully and quickly transfer the burning tinder basket to your kindling. Grin widely and jump around beating your chest; you earned it!

Once Your Fire Is Going:
Memory Verse: Luke 12:34-38

Discuss:
- What it means to be dressed, ready, and to keep the lamps burning.
- How is that different from a servant who is caught napping?
- Why it is important to be a good servant?

Make the Connection

A Service Project

LOCATION:
Pray with your son about having a servant's heart. Fire

gives us warmth, light, comfort and security. Discuss how our service:
- Resembles building a fire.
- Affects others.
- Affects us.

Talk with your son about what gifts and talents you both have. Discuss how your gifts may be used to help and serve others. Discuss how serving others:
- Glorifies God.
- Furthers God's kingdom here on earth.

Based on the gifts and talents you have, identify and plan a service project that you and your son can do together or with other fathers and sons.
- Is there a widow at your church who may need something fixed at her house?
- Is there something you can do at your church (grounds work, painting, etc.)?
- Is there a local food mission that could use financial or food assistance?

FUEL:
Based on where you decided to serve, identify and list what resources from the service triangle will be needed to accomplish your objective.

ORGANIZATION:
Once you have identified your project and what fuel (service triangle) is required, sit down and prayerfully plan out how you will best accomplish the task.
- Do you have adequate resources to accomplish your mission?

- Do you need to enlist the help of friends?
- Have you consulted with the church leadership?

Leadership Note: Make sure to plan out the project with your son. Remember, the more input your son has, the more motivated he will be to complete the task.

IGNITION:

Put it all together and accomplish your mission. Igniting a fire in the wilderness takes effort just like serving others does. May your efforts glorify God and be a blessing to others.

> *His master replied, "Well done, good and faithful servant! You have been faithful with a few things; I will put you in charge of many things. Come and share your master's happiness!"* (Matthew 25:21).

In Matthew 25:14-30, Jesus tells a parable of the master who was leaving on a journey, so he entrusted three of his servants with talents (money) while he was gone. One servant received five talents, one received two talents, and the third servant received one talent. The verses do not say how long the master was to be gone or when he may return. Nor does the master tell his servants what to do with the talents they were given—only that they were entrusted with the talents while the master was gone.

In this account, Jesus makes it clear that God has entrusted each of us with talents—some many and some a few. But what matters to God is not the number of talents we are given; rather, it is how we choose to use them. God expects us to use what we have been given wisely and for the glory of His kingdom.

Chapter 4

Water: Prayer

This, then, is how you should pray: "Our Father in heaven, hallowed be your name, your kingdom come, your will be done on earth as it is in heaven. Give us today our daily bread. Forgive us our debts, as we also have forgiven our debtors. And lead us not into temptation, but deliver us from the evil one" (Matthew 6:9-13).

Several years ago, my friend John and I decided to take our kids on a mountain hike to a scenic overlook. We didn't anticipate any worries; it was only a day hike. I packed a few snacks and a gallon of water for me and my three boys. Without consulting a map, John and I guesstimated the hike to be approximately three miles round trip; this would be easy and we would be back by lunch.

We did not know that the day we chose to hike would end up being the hottest day recorded that summer. Nor did we realize that the overlook was eight miles round trip—on a steep, rugged switch back trail. Sweat poured down our bodies and stung our eyes as we wove our way back and forth up the mountain under that scorching July sun. The heat and humidity were stifling, and our clothes became drenched.

After several hours and numerous water breaks, we reached the overlook. Everybody was exhausted. My second son, Ryan, was six years old at the time. Ryan has always been my "tough guy." Ryan has been blessed with speed, strength, and a spirit that knows neither fear nor defeat; he's had countless stitches to prove it.

Ryan was hurting. His face said it all—the heat, sweat, and mountain were taking their toll even though I had been making sure we stopped and drank often. I knew if Ryan was hurting, the situation was serious. Reaching the overlook took over two hours, and as we gazed at the mountain scenery—mostly obscured by a hot summer haze—I noticed that we were down to one quart of water.

I was concerned and angry with myself. I have seen the effects of dehydration on Marines. I should have been smarter; I knew better. I asked John about his water supply and found out our friends were no better off than we were.

John and I decided to ration the remaining water on the four mile hike back. At about three in the afternoon, it was time to leave, and by now it was really hot. Each child, five total, would get one short drink on breaks. John and I would each get a canteen cap full.

We took our time hiking back down the mountain and through blurry, sweat stung eyes I was careful to watch the kids for signs of heat exhaustion. The hike down the mountain was treacherous—too dangerous for me to carry my four year old, Scott. Halfway down the mountain, I noticed that my boys were tripping and stumbling more often; no one was talking. I had stopped sweating altogether, and the situation was getting dangerous. The almost three hours it took us to get down the mountain seemed like an eternity.

As the summer sun began its descent, my spirits lifted when I saw John's truck. I carefully watched the kids, who did not look well. The mood was capped by lethargy and silence. The drive to the store was made in total silence. No one had the strength or will to talk. What had begun as an easy hike was turned into a hazardous ordeal because of our lack of thorough preparation.

Water

Water is the most abundant element in the human body, making up about 60 percent of our body mass. Depending on climate, altitude, and exertion, the average person can survive up to three days without water.

In the wilderness, several conditions can cause death. Exposure may be the fastest, but dehydration is the sneakiest. You know when you are wet, cold, or hungry; but you must watch closely to determine if you're becoming dehydrated. Dehydration simply means your body is losing more water than it is getting. The three ways our bodies lose water are from sweat, urine, and respiration (breathing).

> **SURVIVAL NOTE**: an adult male is capable of losing over a quart of water through perspiration and respiration every hour.

Dehydration affects every living being that exists on land, and no magic formula can beat it other than simply drinking a lot of water. We all know how important drinking water is when we're hot and sweating, but it is just as important to keep drinking water at the end of the day when you are resting because that is the fluid your body will use to re-plenish your system.

The physiological affects of dehydration can vary slightly from person to person; but in general terms, the initial effects are impatience and headache. As your dehydration worsens, dizziness and confusion follow. This is when the most dangerous aspect of dehydration occurs because you begin to lose self and situational awareness. Everything that follows is a snowball effect leading toward heatstroke and possible death, and you will become powerless to stop it.

> **SURVIVAL NOTE**: Avoid sugary and/or caffeinated drinks because they accelerate dehydration.

Water should always be your first priority when planning activities, and it becomes even more important in the wilderness where water may be hard to find or nonexistent. Keep in mind, water weighs approximately eight pounds per gallon; that is two pounds per quart and can easily become the heaviest item in your pack. Your prior planning coupled with the skills and equipment to find, make, and purify water can save your life.

> **SURVIVAL NOTE**: One simple way to watch for dehydration is to watch your urine. A strong odor or deep yellow to orange color indicates that your body fluid levels are getting low. Urine should be clear to pale yellow and have an undetectable odor.

Pray without ceasing (1 Thessalonians 5:17 NKJV).

One way to assist hydration is to drink by the clock, which simply means picking a time, for example every thirty minutes, and drinking when that time comes—whether you feel thirsty or not. This will ensure a steady flow of vital fluids into the body and reduces the chance of wasting water by binge drinking.

If you drink too much water at one time, your body will not be able to absorb it all, and much of it will come out as waste (urine). In outdoor recreational activities or survival situations, drinking by the clock should become standard operating procedure.

Another help in staying hydrated is to plan before you begin your activity how much water you'll need based on your activity and the climate, so you can ration your water accordingly. This planning will help in many ways. If you estimate ahead of time how much water weight you must carry, you may decide to alter your route or the duration of your activity. You will also know how much water you can use at any given moment.

For our struggle is not against the flesh and blood, but against the rulers, against the authorities, against the powers of this dark world and against the spiritual forces of evil in the heavenly realms (Ephesians 6:12).

As a man becomes dehydrated . . . his courage flows out through his pores, along with his muscular strength. He loses the will to fight or to take constructive action . . . This is not because the voices of conscience and reason don't tell them they are doing wrong, but because they lack the will to respond. In this state of slackness, the attitude of men becomes one of general indifference to the possible consequences of inaction (Col. S.L.A. Marshall).[2]

Spiritual Dehydration

Lives become busy, schedules become cluttered, and before we know it, days, weeks, and even months pass without meaningful communication with God. This is spiritual dehydration, and it comes upon us seemingly without warning. The longer we go without prayer—communication with God—we become indifferent to His plan for our lives. Without notice, we begin to lose the courage to stand firm for His kingdom and grow submissive to the temptations of the world.

As our spiritual dehydration worsens, apathy ensues, leaving us self-absorbed and indifferent to the sin in our lives and in the world around us. The world of right and wrong— the truth of the Word—become shades of gray as worldly values and wisdoms take hold of our hearts. Worse yet, we become confused, disoriented, and careless to the fact that God has a plan for our lives. If we do not reach out to God through prayer and allow Him to lead our hearts and minds, the world will take that leadership role. Whom do you trust?

Yet not as I will, but as you will (Matthew 26:39).

Our spiritual hydration comes from prayer. Just as food/the Word give us strength and energy, prayer gives us courage, resolve, and focus. Prayer is a deliberate act of obedience and humility that keeps our hearts focused on the Lord's will. Numerous accounts are found in the New Testament of Jesus going off to pray by himself. The night before Jesus' crucifixion, knowing what was to come, He went to the garden at Gethsemane and prayed.

Jesus knew that guidance, true courage, and strength can

only come from our Father in heaven. If Jesus, the only Son of the living God, needed to pray then, how much more do we need prayer in our lives?

Do not be anxious about anything, but in everything, by prayer and petition, with thanksgiving, present your requests to God. And the peace of God, which transcends all understanding, will guard your hearts and your minds in Christ Jesus (Philippians 4:6-7).

We are deliberate about staying physically hydrated when we drink by the clock, and we should be deliberate about being spiritually hydrated by establishing regular prayer times throughout our day. Prayer time does not need to be long or eloquent, but it must be consistent and from the heart.

For example, designate five minutes of prayer time when you first wake up in the morning. Once you get into the routine of this, add five minutes at lunch and so on. This will help in many ways. Prayer will keep our minds clear, allowing God to work within us. It will also keep our heart focused on Him so when we are faced with an unexpected crisis or temptation, we can better recognize it and be prepared to respond in a Christ-like way.

Another idea is to create a prayer journal. A prayer journal is a valuable tool designed to reflect the need for God in our lives. A prayer journal is simply a book documenting our thoughts and concerns. It is not a shopping or wish list, but rather our praises, hopes, and concerns written to God about the people, events, and circumstances in our lives.

As time passes and your journal grows, you can review your journal and be rewarded as you document God's answers to those prayers. More often that not, you will notice that God did not answer your prayers in the manner in which you originally hoped, but instead He changed your heart or the way you see the situation.

Water and Wilderness Survival

When it comes to dehydration and wilderness survival, the quest for water can be divided into three basic areas: finding water, making water, and purifying water. We will use these water survival techniques to enhance our prayer life.

SURVIVAL NOTE: All water should be purified before consuming. The purity of water can NEVER be judged by its color, taste, clarity or smell. If you don't have water purification tablets or a water purification system, then the water should be boiled for at least five minutes to ensure that any bacteria or viruses are killed.

Keep in mind that many of the water-born viruses and bacteria take several days to several weeks before they affect the human body. If you have no way of purifying your water, go ahead and drink what is available. Dehydration will kill faster than the viruses can make you sick. To be found alive but sick is far better than to be found dead.

---

1. Finding Water

Terrain:

Water flows downhill, so your best bet is to follow the downward contours of the land. As you work yourself to the lowest geographical point, look for areas where you may be able to dig. Places that have abundant green vegetation or damp soil may indicate hidden water.

Plants:

Several plants store water such as cactus and pine needles. Water can be extracted from the pulp of these plants and supply the body with minimal amounts of fluid. We recommend that you research local plants in your area to determine which ones are available and how best to use them.

Cold Climates:

Dehydration is just as much of a threat in cold climates as it is in hot ones. Snow and ice are made of water and make an obvious, easy solution to your water needs. Whenever possible, care should be taken to melt snow or ice and then boil the water before drinking it. This serves two purposes: first, it ensures that the water you drink is purified; and second, by putting warm fluids into your body you will avoid hypothermia by keeping your core body temperature up where it needs to be.

SURVIVAL NOTE: Melting ice requires less fuel than melting snow.

---

2. Making Water
Mud:

Mud contains water. The trick is to get the water out of the mud. Gravity coupled with a T-shirt, underwear, or any porous fabric will do the trick. So now you know why your mom always told you to wear clean underwear! Take the mud and place it into the fabric in a manner that allows you to squeeze or wring it out of the mud. Make sure you do this over some vessel that will catch the water that drips out. Depending on how "soupy" the mud is, this method can produce a lot of water in a hurry. Obviously, it is very dirty and should always be purified before drinking.

Rain Water:

You can collect rain water if you are prepared with some means of collecting the rain such as a poncho, trash bag, or tent.

Solar Stills:

There are two basic types of solar stills—the above ground still and the below ground still. Solar stills are a very effective way to produce small quantities of drinkable water. But this method requires time, effort, the proper materials, and a lot of sunlight.

SURVIVAL NOTE: Don't wait until you are out of water before attempting this. Assuming you have the proper equipment, it takes a lot of time and produces relatively little water. The time to build a still is before you run out of water.

The Above Ground Still:

All that is required for this still is a large plastic bag, green vegetation, and lots of direct sunlight. The plastic bag

can be placed around the branch of a tree or bush and sealed, or it can be filled with green vegetation and laid directly on the ground, inflated, and sealed. If you place the bag directly on a tree or shrub branch, put a small stone in the bottom of the bag. This will provide a place for the condensed water to pool. Use caution not to tear the bag.

If you place the bag directly on the ground and then fill it with vegetation, make sure you do these three things:

1. Set the bag on a slight hill that is exposed to direct sunlight. This will allow condensation to pool at the bottom. Fill the bag with green vegetation. Try to keep the area where the condensed water pools free of vegetation.

2. Place rocks in the bottom of the bag to keep it in place and assist with drainage.

3. Inflate the bag like a balloon and seal it to ensure the condensation flows properly.

> **SURVIVAL NOTE**: NEVER use poisonous plants in your solar still!

The Below Ground Still:

Equipment Required:

Forty-eight-inch by forty-eight-inch sheet of clear plastic

Cup or vessel to collect the water

Sunlight

A stone

Something to dig with

You will need to dig a hole approximately thirty-six inches in diameter and eighteen inches deep in a location that gets plenty of direct sunlight. If possible, place fresh, green, nonpoisonous plants in the bottom of the hole. Place the cup or vessel in the center of the bottom of the hole (surrounded by the vegetation). Cover the top of the hole with the plastic making sure the center of the plastic hangs down toward the cup at the bottom of the hole (a stone will ensure

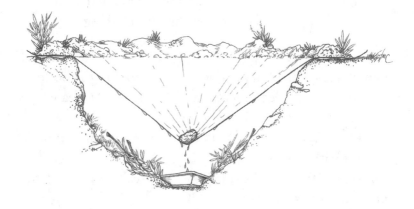

the plastic hangs properly). Finally, create an airtight seal around the edges of the plastic using the freshly dug dirt. (You should carefully consider if the amount of water you collect is worth the sweat you lose.)

3. Purifying Water

Purifying water simply means that you are making water safe to drink by removing contaminants, bacteria, or viruses that can make you sick. The first step is to visually inspect the water to determine if it contains any large pollutants (dirt, plant material, or algae). The second step is to kill any bacteria or viruses in the water.

Step One: Filtering Water

In the absence of a commercially made water filter, the filtering process can be accomplished in two primary ways: run the water through some material that will strain it or allow the water time to sit so that large contaminates settle on the bottom or float to the top to be skimmed off later.

To filter the water, you can use any porous material such as a hat, T-shirt, or even your underwear. If you have access to wood, charcoal, sand, or fine gravel, you can use it to increase the effectiveness of your filtering process. Allowing water to sit and settle is time-consuming and requires two water containers—one to let the water settle and one into which to pour the settled water.

Step Two: Purifying Water

Regardless of how clear or clean the water appears, you must purify it to kill any viruses or bacteria that may be present. The three primary ways we can do this are boiling, using chemical purification tablets, or using commercial purification filters.

Boiling:
There are two basic ways to boil water. The first method simply involves putting the water into a flame resistant container and placing that container directly over a heat source until the water boils. The second technique involves filling something with water (a boot, a thick cotton hat, or some other material capable of holding water) and placing a heated object into the water.

Lining a hole in the ground with water resistant material (blanket, buckskin, or clay) will also work. And by making a larger hole and utilizing larger rocks, you can purify a larger quantity of water. This method requires more time and effort but is effective. Use caution when placing hot rocks into water as some heated rocks may pop or explode on contact with the water.

Purification Tablets:
Everyone should have water purification tablets in their wilderness survival kits. These are readily available in most stores that sell camping or survival gear. I don't make a specific recommendation on any brand but whatever you purchase, make sure you know how to use the tablets properly before you need them. Tablets require time to work—some take thirty minutes before the water can be consumed.

Purification Filters:
The big advantage of purification filters is that they can purify water instantly. The down side is that they are often

expensive and some are bulky, although most weigh very little.

SURVIVAL NOTE: A degree of redundancy will serve you well. A large piece of clear plastic or plastic trash bag, water purification tablets, a purification filter, and a small metal cup could all be in your survival pack to ensure that you would be prepared for any water crisis.

Finding Prayer Time

And pray in the Spirit on all occasions with all kinds of prayers and requests (Ephesians 6:18).

Life is busy, and prayer requires time and effort. Nevertheless, praying is the most important thing you will do in any day. We discussed drinking by the clock earlier; the same principle works for prayer. God wants to hear from you—not just when you are experiencing hard times. Be deliberate about prayer time. Unfortunately, many people are more concerned about missing baseball practice or their tee time than praying to their Creator.

It can be very helpful to have a prayer partner. A prayer partner is simply a friend that you pray with at regular times. A prayer partner will add accountability and support.

Praying

But when you pray, go into your room, close the door and pray to your Father, who is unseen (Matthew 6:6).

The first step in prayer is to recognize that you need to pray. This sounds silly, but your acknowledgement that you need to pray reflects your humility and obedience to God. If you have questions about how you should pray, all you need to do is open your Bible. In Mathew 6:5-13, Jesus explains exactly how a person should and should not pray.

What prayer is:
- A dialog with our Creator, fellowship with our heavenly Father.
- A deliberate act of submission, a time to humble ourselves.
- An act of adoration for the Creator of all things, a time to give thanks.
- An opportunity to repent for sin in our lives.
- An opportunity to lift up concerns we may have.

What prayer is not:
- An opportunity to counsel God or give Him advice.
- An immediate panacea.
- A shopping list or a wish list.

Purifying Prayer

The end of all things is near. Therefore be clear minded and self-controlled so that you can pray (1 Peter 4:7).

Meaningful prayer is a deliberate act of worship, submission, and obedience. It is how we talk to God. Praying with purpose takes practice; we can often become distracted. What we need to do first when we pray is to filter out the distractions or contaminants in our minds. The contaminants are those extraneous thoughts that pop into our minds and keep us from fully focusing our hearts and attention on God.

Simply opening up our Bibles and reading a few verses helps us keep a proper focus. Highlighting those verses that have impacted our lives in a significant way can be helpful. They can also be written in the back of a prayer journal. Another way to filter out the contaminants is to take a moment and be still.

Once we have our minds clear and our hearts focused on God, we need to praise and give thanks to our Father for all the He has done in our lives. Next, we should examine our hearts and repent for the sin in our lives. We boil water to remove unseen things that can make us sick, and we examine our hearts and repent to ensure that our prayers will be unhindered. If we do this, we can approach God with humility and honesty.

Be mindful that prayer is a personal conversation we have with God. Be sure to let Him have an opportunity to speak and be prepared to obey when He does. Quality prayer, like any skill, takes practice; the more we practice, the better it gets.

Practice Your Survival Skills

As with any survival skill, we strongly recommend that you practice the skills and techniques before you need them. Nevertheless, water is essential for life; and drinking unpurified water can lead to a variety of illnesses. When practicing these skills, always make certain you have enough clean water to drink. Water produced or purified through the following methods should not be consumed unless you are in a real survival situation.

Find Water
Time required: TBD
Equipment Required:
Bible
Something to dig with
Memory Verse: 1 Thessalonians 5:17-18

Take a hike in the wilderness to look for possible sources of water. Make careful observation of the terrain and vegetation, and discuss where you may be able to look for water. On your hike, practice drinking by the clock. Every time you stop to take a drink, take a moment to reflect on a blessing in your life; give thanks for it.

Discuss:
- What it means to have a thankful heart, and list some reasons you are thankful.
- Some ways you can pray more often.
- Ways to establish routine prayer times.

Make Water: (Solar still)
Time required: 4-8 hours
Equipment Required:
Bible
Forty-eight-inch by forty-eight-inch sheet of plastic
Plastic garbage bag
Shovel
Metal cup

Find a spot that gets a lot of direct sunlight. Dig a hole in the ground approximately thirty-six inches in diameter and eighteen inches deep. Take your cup and place it at the bottom in the center of the hole. Surround the cup with fresh, green, nonpoisonous vegetation. Place the plastic over the hole and put the stone in the center of the plastic. Allow the stone on the plastic to drop directly over—but not into—the cup. Ensure the outer edges of the plastic completely cover the hole, and seal or cover the edges of the plastic with the remaining dirt.

Once this is done, all you need to do is wait for the sun to "cook" the moisture out of the soil and vegetation. When the vapor hits the plastic, it will condense and begin dripping down into the cup.

SURVIVAL NOTE: NEVER use poisonous plants in your solar still!

Once you have completed the below ground still, construct an above ground still. Find a tree branch or shrub that gets lots of direct sunlight. Place the bag over the branch, getting as many leaves inside as possible. Place a stone in the bottom of the bag. Seal the bag around the branch with rope. After several hours, measure the amount of water you have collected in both stills.

Read: Read Matthew 6:5-13
Discuss:
• How does Jesus say we should pray?
• How does Jesus say we should not pray?
• Things we should and should not pray for.

SURVIVAL NOTE: It is wise to keep leather work gloves in your kit.

Purifying Water: (Rocks)
Time required: 2 hours
Equipment Required:
Bible
Old boot, cotton hat, or a vessel that can contain water
Stones or rocks
Sticks (for moving hot rocks)
A fire
Source of water
Safety glasses*

Get a fire going and place several rocks into the coals (this would be a perfect time to practice your fire making skills). Allow plenty of time for the rocks to become hot. Fill an old boot or hat with water you want to purify. Once the rocks or stones have heated up, put on your safety glasses* and carefully use the sticks to place the stones into the water. Once the stones begin to cool, replace them with stones fresh from the fire and repeat as required.

*You probably won't have safety glasses in a real survival situation, but practice safety.

Read: Psalm 66: 18-19
Discuss:
• What does the psalmist say about keeping unconfessed sin in our hearts?

- Why is it important to confess and repent of our sins before asking God for blessings?

Make the Connection

Pray Together

Designate a specific time to pray together with your son— perhaps before bed or school each day. It is important that you keep this time special as it is a great opportunity to spend time connecting with your son and with God. Identify a location that affords limited interruptions and distractions.

Prayer Journals

A great way to connect with your son is to make a prayer journal with him. The journal can be as simple or as elaborate as you like. You can use anything from scraps of paper stapled together to commercially manufactured prayer journals that are sold at your local Christian bookstore.

After you have discussed those items that are often on your hearts and would like each other to pray for, document them in your journal. This may consist of the following:

- Family members and other people the Lord has brought into your life such as friends, teachers, and missionaries you support. Don't forget to pray for those God has placed in authority over us such as church leaders and government officials.
- Give thanks to God for the blessings—both large and small—in your lives.
- Identify areas of sin that are a struggle for you.
- Wrong thinking that needs to be overcome.
- Issues that cause concern and decisions that need to be made.

Update your journal as needed and document answers to your prayers. Use your Bible to seek out and record Scripture verses that apply to your prayer requests.

When he finished, one of his disciples said to him, "Lord, teach us to pray, just as John taught his disciples" (Luke 11:1).

How many times have you told your son, "You need to pray about [you fill in this blank]." That is a true statement, but you must realize that your son may not know exactly how he should pray. Your son learns how to pray by listening to and watching you pray. You must always be ready to guide his thoughts by guiding his words. By helping to guide your son's thoughts you help him to understand what godly blessings are and are not.

Finally, you can never expect your son to humble himself before God if he has never seen you do it. By regularly praying with your son you show him your heart, guide his thinking, and create a godly ripple that will continue for generations.

Chapter 5

Food: The Word of God

*These commandments that I give you today are to be upon
your hearts. Impress them on your children. Talk about
them when you sit at home and when you walk along the
road, when you lie down and when you get up*
(Deuteronomy 6:6-7).

"Now sit down and pay attention," Tim said as he began a
thirty minute safety briefing. "Your ability to observe what's
going on around you may prevent an accident or even save a
life," he said as he studied the faces of the twelve young men.
The twelve adventurers' reasons for coming to a Christian
leadership camp varied, but at this particular time, they all
had one thing in common: they were more concerned with
maintaining their tough guy appearance than anything a
tattoo-covered, long-haired Christian counselor had to say.

As Tim spoke the other counselor, Chuck, stood silently
watching. Chuck's outward appearance was the polar opposite of Tim. Chuck was a clean-cut Lieutenant in the U.S.
Air Force. Nevertheless, both men were resolute on their purpose for being at Wilderness Camp. They had three weeks,
two hundred miles of hard trails, and the Word of God to
turn these twelve individual boys into a team of godly young
men.

Without warning, Tim and Chuck just took off running.
They simply said, "Follow us" and started jogging up the trail.
The boys quickly snapped out of their self-absorbed reflec-
tions and found themselves frantically trying to follow their
leaders. It was every man for himself as they struggled in
vain, trying to catch up with their leaders.

Just as quickly as the run began, it ended. Huffing and

puffing, eleven young men straggled up to the summit of Tip Top, the highest peak on camp property. As the young men arrived, they found Tim and Chuck clad in shorts and running shoes, quietly talking and drinking bottled water.

It was at this moment that each camper began to recall that, during the Basic Safety Lecture, Tim and Chuck removed their jeans and hiking boots and replaced them with shorts and running shoes. How could something as strange as two grown men changing clothes—right in front of them—go unnoticed? It was Chuck who presented the second lecture of the day, but the first that the campers actually heard.

"What was the first thing Tim and I instructed you to do this morning?" Although it was not rhetorical, the question went unanswered by the eleven boys that had made it to the summit. Chuck filled in the dead air that seemed to linger a few moments too long. "Based on the fact that you boys are still wearing street clothes tells me you may need to hear the first lesson again."

This time twenty-two ears eagerly listened for the words of wisdom that they had missed earlier. Then in a voice close to a whisper Tim said, "Observe, Observe, Observe." Without explanation or elaboration, the two leaders took off running back down the hill and out of sight.

Nourishment

You have heard the old saying, "Give a man a fish and he will eat for a day, but teach a man how to fish and he will eat for a lifetime." For your body, food is energy, stamina, and strength to grow and fight off disease and sickness. A typical person can live three to four weeks without food before disease and subsequent death ensue.

The body must be fed, and something happens when it is not; it begins to consume itself. The body's ability to temporarily cannibalize itself was designed to allow us to survive brief times of famine until life sustaining food could be acquired. If nourishment cannot be obtained, weakness, disease, and death will follow.

Today your need for food can be satisfied with a short walk to the fridge or a quick trip to a restaurant. People take for granted that not only will they eat every day, but they will have unlimited choices in what they eat. In a wilderness survival situation, no such luxury of quantity, convenience, or choice is available. You eat what the season and your geographic location dictate; that is, assuming you have the knowledge of the items that are edible and the skills to obtain them.

Food is all about providing the strength and the energy to survive; taste has little to do with it. To understand this, all you need to do is observe the animals that live in the wild. From squirrels to bears, all creatures know that there will be times of feast and lean times of famine. Every fall, creatures are busy storing food and fat, preparing themselves for long, cold winters. Those creatures lacking the ability to store food and fat leave the area, migrating toward warmer climates.

Fortunately, God created man to be omnivorous, giving us the ability to eat animals and plants, which greatly improves the chances for success and survival at all times of year and in all places. However, unlike the animals, you have no such ability to predict the "winters"—those hard times in your life. It will be your ability to identify, locate, and gather food in preparation for them that may make the difference between life and death.

Wilderness survival foods can generally be divided into two categories: plants and animals.

Plants: It is estimated that just over one third of the known species of plant are edible, and in most places in the world they are abundant.[3] Plants may be abundant, but with the exception of nuts, plants have the lowest caloric density, meaning you'll need to eat a lot of them. Additionally, some plants if eaten can cause sickness or death, so we must have the ability to identify those edibles from the poisonous ones.

Animals: Regardless of where in this world you are, animals exist, and mammals, birds, fish, and reptiles can provide needed sustenance and energy if you know how to harvest and prepare them. Keep in mind, protein dense foods require the body to use more water to digest properly. Insects are found almost everywhere in the world, and many are edible, providing a good source of protein and calories.

The two primary issues when it comes to insects are the fact that they're small and well, they're bugs. When you look at both factors together, you realize that you may have to eat a lot of them if that is the only food source.

SURVIVAL NOTE: Edible food items may not always look, smell, or taste good or be easy to swallow; but our lives may depend on the nutrition and energy they provide.

As a father, you understand the critical importance of training your son before adversity strikes. Countless resources are available to aid in the identification of both edible and poisonous plants. Your prior study and preparation will be directly proportional to your chances of surviving. Many items may appear tasty and edible but in reality are poisonous and/or potentially deadly. (The third chapter of Genesis highlights this well.)

It would be impossible to attempt to identify everything in this world that is edible and poisonous in this short book, and with plants the task becomes even more complicated. For example, all parts of the dandelion are edible, whereas only parts of the wild rhubarb may be eaten. Fortunately almost every mammal, bird, and fish can be eaten.

So how do you determine what is good for food and what is not? Simply—one bite at a time. Start small. You do this by observation, interpretation and application. You need to make careful observations before you can interpret what you have found to be edible or poisonous. After you have accurately identified what you harvested, you can apply it (utilize it to meet your need).

SURVIVAL NOTE: If you are unaware of any edible plants in your region, simply surf the Internet or go to your library with your son and research them. If you begin by identifying a few edible plants, you can more easily identify other plants that may be similar.

Be still, and know that I am God; I will be exalted among the nations, I will be exalted in the earth (Psalm 46:10).

Observation is the first step toward finding food in the wilderness. Start by looking at the big picture and asking the big and broad questions. This is a fairly quick and simple task, requiring little more than taking a moment to evaluate your surroundings: stop, look, and listen. The longer you are still and quiet, the more the forest will come to life and unveil itself. Some of these big questions may be:

- What type of terrain (mountains, desert, tropical, or tundra) am I on?

  The type of terrain you are on will give a good indication as to what sort of plants and animals may be present.

- What season is it? Many animals become scarce in the winter and plants are in hibernation.

- Do I see evidence of water? All living things need water to survive. Locating a source of water will most often lead to the discovery of edible plants and animals.

- Is one plant or animal abundant in the area?

You may wish to identify the most abundant possible food item first. Expending a large amount of energy, time, and materials to making weapons to hunt dear would be silly if you are near a stream that is teaming with trout.

Now, begin to narrow your observations by focusing on specific details (plants or animals):

- Look for things that attract your attention. What obvious feature makes it conspicuous? This is often a unique color, odor, or unusual shape or size.

- Note patterns. This could be patterns of leaves on a plant or petals on a flower.

- Game trails. Can you identify animal tracks (hoofs or claws)? Note the shape, size, color, texture, odor, location, and content of feces.

- Note those things that are common to all living beings. Most living things have a few fundamental needs— food, water, shelter, and protection. Recognizing how your specimen meets these basic needs may go a long way in identifying it and ultimately harvesting it.

The keys to making good observations are patience and practice. Now that you have made careful observation, you need to interpret what that knowledge means. In other words, "Can I eat it or some portion of it?" If the answer is yes, you should still exercise caution in most cases as the food may be new to your system.

However, if after careful observation of a plant you still can't interpret if it's edible, use a field test for plants because you do not want to risk poisoning yourself by eating something toxic. The field test is based on a series of observations and interpretations.

Begin by making careful visual observations of the plant. If it looks edible, crush up a small portion of the plant and rub it on a sensitive spot on your skin (wrists, neck) and wait five minutes. If you DO NOT have any reaction such as burning, itching, or hives, then place a small portion of the plant in your mouth but DO NOT swallow it! Leave the plant material in your mouth for at least five minutes. If you detect no burning, itching, or other unpleasant sensation after five minutes, swallow the plant material and wait at least eight hours. It is important that you do not eat or drink anything else during this period.

If you experience no adverse reactions (cramps, nausea, or diarrhea), take about a half cup full and eat it; wait another eight hours. If you suffer no side effects, the plant can be considered safe to eat. Keep in mind that even though you have determined this is safe to eat, it is still new to your system and should be eaten in moderation until you become used to it.[4]

> **SURVIVAL NOTE**: When field testing plants, pick one part of the plant—the part you think may be edible—and stay with that part. Remember, just because the flower petals may be edible DOES NOT mean the leaves are.

Now that you have interpreted the meaning of your observations, it's time to figure out how you are going to apply it to meet your need or harvest it for your use. Some food items may need to be cooked before eating. Other food items may present unique harvesting challenges.

Here is where you look at your equipment and inventory your resources. You don't want to expend more energy getting the food than the food itself provides or risk injury in attempting to harvest it. A bow is better than a spear; a trap is better than both. With some animals there is a risk to benefit ratio: if you find yourself in an area that abounds with skunk, which are edible, perhaps you should continue your search for other food items unless you're really, really hungry.

Likewise, if all you're equipped with is a knife and homemade spear, perhaps deer hunting should not be undertaken. The amount of energy or calories you will expend attempting to hunt deer is probably not worth the gamble. Some questions you may want to ask yourself are:

• What is the most efficient way of harvesting it?

- Can it be trapped?
- If I do catch it, is it dangerous?
- Does it need to be cooked?
- Can I gather and store it or will it spoil?

SURVIVAL NOTE: All meat and insects should be thoroughly cooked before eaten. Many animals carry disease or parasites that can make you sick.

It is written: "Man does not live on bread alone, but on every word that comes from the mouth of God" (Matthew 4:4).

Fuel for Spiritual Growth

Just as food provides the fuel to grow and the energy to sustain your daily activities and fight off disease, the Word of God provides the fuel for spiritual growth, which sustains you as you travel through a hostile, wicked world and is your chief defense against sin and temptation. Sin is like a disease that infects our hearts, stifling your fellowship with God. The Word of God is the armor of God.

When Jesus was tempted by Satan in the wilderness, He resisted the devil with the truth of Scripture. Satan's primary weapon against the children of God is his ability to deceive. When you study God's Word, you become more aware of who God is and what He has done for you. Not only do you gain strength and stamina for resisting disease (temptation and sin), you become more observant—able to recognize what should and should not be allowed into your heart and life.

Your spirit must be fed, and something begins to happen when it is not; you may become self-consumed. If your son is not trained with the skills and ability to harvest the Word for himself, he will become desperate to fill the void within him—willing to ingest anything in this world that looks good and not knowing if it's toxic until it's already inside his heart and mind.

> *For the word of God is living and active. Sharper than any double-edged sword, it penetrates even to dividing soul and spirit, joints and marrow; it judges the thoughts and attitudes of the heart* (Hebrews 4:12).

For many, spiritual sustenance is satisfied with a quick trip to the local church. By physically being there, some feel that they have provided their family with all the nourishment they need to grow in the Lord. Even if you attend a church that diligently preaches the Word of God, you may still be depending too much on someone else for your spiritual nourishment. Remember, as a father you alone are ultimately responsible for the spiritual training of your son—not your pastor; not your son's Sunday school teacher, and not his mother. The Great Commission begins in your house!

> *Like newborn babies, crave pure spiritual milk, so that by it you may grow up in your salvation* (1 Peter 2:2).

When it comes to food in a survival situation, you don't have the luxury of quantity, convenience, or choice. You will need the skills to harvest life-sustaining food for yourself. You must have the knowledge to not only discern what is edible from what is poisonous, but also the skills to harvest those foods.

Everything in the Bible is "edible" and nutritious, but you must have the skills to harvest the spiritually sustaining Word of God for yourself or it will be of little value to you.

He satisfies the thirsty and fills the hungry with good things (Psalm 107:9).

Good Bible study, like everything else, should begin with prayer. Ask God to open your eyes, heart, and mind to the truth of His Word. The Bible consists of multiple books and thousands of pages. So where do you begin? The answer is simple—one verse at a time. You do this by observation, interpretation, and application.[5]

Observation is what you see.
Interpretation is what it means.
Application is how it applies to your life.

Your observations of the Bible are the first steps toward feeding your spirit "the pure spiritual milk." And just as everything else in life, the strength of anything depends on the solidness of its foundation. When you make observations, what you are really doing is being a detective by identifying as many facts and details as possible.

Depending on the age of your son, begin by picking a book, chapter, or verse and read it through in one sitting. Get out a notepad and start by looking at the big picture, asking the big and broad questions. Some of these big questions may be:

- Am I reading from the New Testament or the Old Testament?
- Who is the author?
- What genre or type of literature is it? (We don't read poetry the same way we read a narrative or prophetic literature.)
- What is the main idea of the book or the story?
- Does the author state his purpose in the text?

SURVIVAL NOTE: Some versions of the Bible may be too difficult for your son to understand. You may consider a children's story Bible or a version that is age appropriate.

After you have completely read through your chosen book, chapter, or verse one time, try to narrow your observations by noting:
- Things that stand out: names of people, locations (nations, cities, towns) that are noted in the Bible.
- Look for patterns. Is a word or phrase repeated?
- Note events or circumstances. What did they do or fail to do? What was God's response?

Then Philip ran up to the chariot and heard the man reading Isaiah the prophet. "Do you understand what you are reading?" Philip asked. "How can I," he said, "unless someone explains it to me?" (Acts 8:30-31).

Once you have documented all of your observations, it's time to interpret their meaning. Good interpretation begins with—you guessed it—prayer. Examine your observations and ask God for wisdom and understanding. Meditate on the Word and do not make assumptions.

SURVIVAL NOTE: The better and more detailed your observations, the easier it will be to interpret meaning. Be careful when you ask, "What does this mean?" You need to focus on what God intended it to mean—not what you want or hope it means.

When interpreting Scripture, you may need to compare verse against verse for a broader perspective. Describing an entire forest based on the observation of a single tree is impossible. However, if after making careful observations of Scripture you are still not quite sure how to interpret its meaning, you will need to research it further.

Regardless of how hungry you were, you would not feel comfortable eating a berry if the only observations made were that the bush it came from had green leaves.

The Bible is the Word of God, and you do not need to apply any field test to it. However, to fully and correctly understand the meaning of Scripture, you may consider the use of one or more of the following:

- Study Bible
- Commentary
- Concordance
- Bible dictionary
- Bible atlas
- Bible handbook

Just like plant and animal guides in the wilderness, these biblical reference tools will be invaluable in your quest to understand the Word of God.

SURVIVAL NOTE: Even if you are confident you understand pieces of Scripture, spend time researching them with your son. This is quality time and a good training opportunity for him.

Do not merely listen to the word, and so deceive yourselves. Do what it says (James 1:22).

Our application of the Word is where the rubber meets the road. Application simply means "How do I apply this to my life?" For some people this may be the most challenging part of Bible study. To aid in the application of the Word, you may want to start by simply asking yourself:
- Is there something I should do?
- Is there something to avoid?

SURVIVAL NOTE: Sometimes God's Word may be "hard to swallow" and force us to examine and change our attitudes, opinions, and behavior. But it is the only way we can grow in the Lord and gain spiritual strength and energy.

Practice Your Survival Skills

> **SURVIVAL NOTE**: As with any survival skill we strongly recommend that you practice the skills before you need them. Food is essential for life, but you should never ingest anything unless you have positively identified it and are absolutely sure that it's safe to eat.

Make Observations

Time Required: one to two hours
Equipment Required:
- Bible
- Notepad and pen
- Magnifying glass
- Plant identification book for your region
- Animal identification book
- Camera

Plan a trip with your son to a local park, the forest, or any wilderness area. Bring snacks and water, and plan to make it a fun day of discovery. Start small—mark an area of about fifty square paces and work within this site.

Make Observations:
Begin by asking big questions and record these in the notebook. Here are just a few to get you started:

- What time of day is it?
- What time of year (season) is it.

- What is the weather?
- What do you see, hear, and smell?

Narrow Your Observations:
- How many different animals or evidence of animals do you see?
- How many different plants do you see?
- Can you find insects?

Take your magnifying glass, camera, notebook, and plant/animal identification books, and begin to identify what you see. Take your time and study each item carefully by comparing and contrasting it to what is recorded in your books.

Make Interpretations Based on Your Observations:
Begin to identify what is edible and what is not. If you still are not sure, take a small sample home and research it further with your son. If it's an animal, take photos of it and only bring the pictures home.

Apply It To Your Use:
Once you have identified as many edible food items as possible, discuss how you would harvest them and/or prepare them for consumption. Plants need to be harvested, and animals hunted or trapped; discuss strategies for each and create a list of items you may want to ensure you keep in your survival kit to make harvesting easier.

Memory Verse: Psalm 46:10 (read the entire psalm).
Discuss:
- Why was this psalm written?

• What is the purpose of this psalm?
• How can I apply verse 10 to my life?

Build a Bow and Arrow

Time Required: one to two hours
Equipment Required:
• Bible
• Knife
• Cordage
• Feather

Plan a hike with your son. Before you leave, research what wood is common in your area and good for bow making.

Leadership Note: Making bows and arrows is as much art as it is a science. Be as technical as you desire, but the point here is that your son will have fun and gain confidence in his new skill. You will want to research primitive bows or self bows to learn some basics before you begin.

Once you have identified the wood you want to use, begin shaping your bow. Depending on the age of your son, you may want to allow him to practice his skills with a knife and help in the process. Once you have fashioned your bow, take your cordage and string it; give a few test pulls to ensure it's safe and won't break. This may take a few attempts before you get a workable bow.

Now unstring your bow and begin fashioning an arrow. The straighter the shaft you begin with, the easier it will be. Once you have fashioned your arrow, set up a target and practice with your bow.

Memory verse: Deuteronomy 8:1-5

Discuss:
- Who is the author of these verses?
- Why did God cause the Israelites to experience hunger?
- What lesson did hunger teach the Israelites?

Build a Spring Snare Trap

Time Required: one hour
Equipment Required:
- Bible
- Knife
- Cordage

Numerous variations of snare traps can be built with little equipment, effort, and time. The spring snare trap is probably one of the easiest traps to make. It requires minimal effort and material, and is relatively quick to make. However, its use

is generally restricted to smaller game unless you really know what you're doing.

The hard part is identifying a viable game trail. Identifying a game trail may test your ability to observe trails through the forest or camouflaged dens.

SURVIVAL NOTE: Try to keep your scent off the trail as much as possible. For many animals, smell is their dominant sense. If the animal smells your odor on the trail, it may alter its course.

Now, take a stick or something to simulate an animal and test your trap.

Memory verse: 2 Timothy 3:16-17

Discuss:

• What does the apostle Paul say is the source of Scripture?

• What can we use Scripture for?

• Why does a godly man need to know Scripture?

Make the Connection:

Fathers, do not exasperate your children; instead, bring them up in the training and instruction of the Lord (Ephesians 6:4).

A Father/Son Bible Study

Begin by choosing one book in the Bible. The Gospels are a great place to start. Designate a specific time and location for your Bible study. Perhaps coincide this with your prayer time.

Remember, the more you practice, the better you will become. Depending on the age of your son, you may read an entire book or just a few chapters.

Make observations:
• Who wrote the book?
• Who is the intended audience?
• Who is the book about?

Make interpretations:
• What is the purpose of the book?
• Is there a central message or theme?

Apply it to your life:
• Is there anything I need to do?
• Is there anything I need to avoid?

Leadership Note: the depth of your study should be based on your son's age and ability.

Whatever you have learned or received or heard from me, or seen in me—put into practice. And the God of peace will be with you (Philippians 4:9).

Challenges that are prepared for are already half overcome. None of you can predict your son's future with one exception—one day he will walk out of your house and into the wilderness we call the world, and you won't be there to guide him. Where will he find spiritual strength and nourishment? By teaching your son the basic skills to make good biblical observations, the knowledge to interpret its meaning, and subsequently apply Scripture to his life, you will help to clothe your son in the full armor of God.

The time to train is now, for when the hard times come, it may be too late. Studying the Bible with your son takes time, but this quality time spent with your son is introducing him to God. Teach your son to fish, and he will eat for a lifetime.

Chapter 6

Shelter in Fellowship

Though one may be overpowered, two can defend them-selves. A cord of three strands is not quickly broken (Ecclesiastes 4:12).

Edward never reached the summit of Tip Top. He never learned the lesson on the imperatives of making observations. If he had, he would have changed out of his hiking boots and into running shoes. But running in heavy boots was not the major factor in Edward's failure to reach the summit. Physically, Edward was the strongest camper on the trip. But for all of the strength in his arms and legs, his pride was stronger; he would never ask for help.

Edward was halfway up the mountain when Tim and Charles passed him on their way down. Before Edward could turn himself around, nine campers passed him by hot on the trail of their two leaders. Edward almost had the humility and courage to ask where they were headed, but that would show weakness.

Thirty minutes into the trip, Edward's feet were covered with blisters. He was hot, thirsty, and overdressed. As the last two boys passed by without acknowledging his presence, Edward's pride unleashed frustration as he said, "I quit!" Edward walked back to camp; he no longer noticed the blisters on his feet or the mosquitoes biting his flesh. His pride was hurt, and it weighed him down as if he were carrying a load of bricks.

The other boys experienced the same conditions as Edward but kept going. As the campers pushed themselves closer to exhaustion, shouts of encouragement began to fill the air. Even a short legged, slightly overweight boy pushed harder and faster with each shout of encouragement. The more a camper seemed to struggle, the louder his friends would yell.

When they arrived back behind the dining hall and saw their leaders sitting on the pile of gear and backpacks, they each felt as if they had just won the Super Bowl. No one noticed that Edward was gone and was now sitting on the steps of the camp director's office, waiting for a ride home.

An hour later they were separated into small groups and had to divide and carry three weeks worth of food and equipment. Edward's absence was now noticed as the load he would have carried was now spread among his teammates.

Edward refused support from the rest of the group and quickly found himself alone and exposed—overwhelmed by the adversity that faced him. The other eleven boys found encouragement from a brother in Christ; it was all they needed to keep going. They found shelter in each other and overcame feelings of fatigue and frustration. They conquered adversity together until they reached their objective.

Shelter

In a survival situation, exposure to the elements can kill you in as few as three hours—faster than dehydration or starvation can. Just as a roof and walls help you to weather the storms of this world, your fellowship with other believers helps to weather the storms of life. Whether you're lost in the wilderness or facing a life crisis, your ability to find or build shelter can mean the difference between life and death.

To understand the basics of shelter building—regardless of how you build your shelter—you need to know four important considerations for shelter: location, foundation, orientation, and resources.

Location

Whether in the wilderness or the world, you know how important it is to observe, observe, observe. Keep a watchful eye out for preexisting, natural features such as caves, overhangs, or fallen trees that require the least amount of effort or modification for shelter. Once you think you have a good location, take a moment and look around. Terrain, trees, and shrubs can tell you a lot about your location.

Terrain

Cold air flows downhill; warm air flows up. Avoid building your shelter at the lowest geographical point. Wherever water is, you can bet that it's also at the lowest geographical point in that specific location. A mere ten feet in elevation can make a huge difference in air temperature. However, building your shelter at the highest point may not be wise either as this may expose your shelter to higher winds.

One exception to this is if you find yourself in an area where mosquitoes and biting flies are prevalent. In that case you may want to shelter where a breeze is present. If possible, find a spot somewhere in the middle. This will keep you above the coldest air, allow you to take advantage of rising air thermals, and keep you out of the strongest winds.

Trees and Shrubs

If the majority of trees/shrubs bend in a certain direction, it may be an indicator of the predominate winds in that location.

A few additional factors need to be considered concerning the location of your shelter. Although being near water is desirable for drinking, cooking, and cleaning, it does pose a few hazards. If you are near water, situate your shelter well above the highest watermarks.

SURVIVAL NOTE: Never build your shelter in a dry stream bed!

Flash floods and rising water can cause you to lose valuable equipment, deny you access to a desired location, cause injury, or even result in death. Also avoid situating your camp on a well-traveled game trail; the presence of game may indicate predators.

Foundation

God's Word speaks a great deal about the importance of a solid foundation and for good reason. You want to know what is underneath you, and you don't want surprises.

Now that you have chosen the location for your shelter, take a stick and clear away leaves and debris from your shelter site. This will help to remove creatures that bite or sting. By using a stick to clear your site, you minimize the risk of being bitten, stung, or cutting your hand, which may lead to other serious problems. Next, depending on your site location, you may consider taking a rock or stick and digging a drainage trench around your shelter to direct water away from your shelter, keeping your bedding dry.

Never, if at all possible, sleep on exposed ground.

Sleeping on the bare soil will suck the heat right out of your body. Use leaves, pine boughs, pine needles, or moss to create a bed at least six inches thick when compressed.

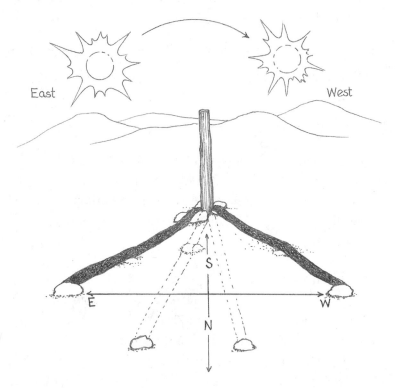

Orientation

Whenever possible, orient the front of your shelter towards the sun: east-southeast. The proper orientation will take full advantage of the suns warming effects by giving you the best exposure to the sun first thing in the morning when it's coldest. Also, storms typically come in from the westnorthwest. It is best, if possible, to have the back of your shelter to the storm and your face to the sun.

> **SURVIVAL NOTE**: To determine direction without a compass, take a straight stick, about eighteen inches long and place it vertically in the ground. Look for the point on the ground where the tip of the stick's shadow is; mark that point with a stone. Wait about thirty minutes; now look for the point on the ground where the tip of the stick's shadow is; mark the second point with a stone. Draw a line between the stones; this is your east-west line. Now, draw a bisecting line, perpendicular to your east-west line; this is north-south.

Resources

The resources you have available depend on two things: what you brought with you and what natural resources—based on your specific location and environment—you have readily available. Inventory your resources: What EQUIPMENT did you bring with you? Are you wearing underwear? Do you have shoelaces? The band from your underwear or shoelaces makes excellent cordage for building your shelter. Do you really need to wear underwear in a survival situation?

> **SURVIVAL NOTE**: One easy method to ensure you always have enough cordage: replace your hiking boot laces with 550 (Para) cord, which is comprised of several individual, strong nylon inner cords surrounded by a nylon sheath. In an emergency you can take the 550 cord off your boots, use the inner cords to build your shelter, and replace the sheath for boot laces (to keep your underwear on!).

Have a PLAN. Be creative but frugal. In a survival situation you can't afford to waste precious resources that include calories and sweat. The better prepared you are with equipment, the less time and effort you will have to expend. Obviously, different geographic areas offer vastly different building resources; it is vitally important that you are familiar with what is available where you are and know how to maximize its use.

The type of shelter you need is determined by your EVALUATION—observation of geographic location, time of year, and weather. The shelter you build will be determined by the equipment or resources you have available as well as your imagination.

SURVIVAL NOTE: If you find yourself exposed and completely lacking resources, you may have to search for better ground. Before you begin your search, ensure that you prayerfully consider the direction of your search and thoroughly evaluate your surroundings before departing.

Once you have determined what type of shelter to build, you need to consider the following:

- Framework: ensure the framework of your shelter is sturdy enough to hold the weight of any additional insulating material. Also consider snow or ice as an additional weight possibility.
- Precipitation: can your shelter protect you from rain, snow or sleet?
- Oxygen: is there adequate ventilation in your shelter?

- Wind: does your shelter keep the wind out?
- Insulation: does your shelter provide enough insulation above, below, and around you to keep you from freezing?
- Fire: ensure that your shelter is a safe distance from your fire.

SURVIVAL NOTE: In cold climates you can use sticks to take rocks heated by your fire and move them into your shelter; the rocks act as portable heaters and will not catch anything on fire.

He who walks with the wise grows wise, but a companion of fools suffers harm (Proverbs 13:20).

All of you know the sheer power of peer pressure and are rightfully concerned. Friends and associations can provide wise counsel, needed comfort, and timely encouragement; or they can drag you down to dark and stormy places. Just as exposure to the elements can rapidly bring physical death, exposure to negative influences can rapidly kill your spirit. Without question, one of the most important lessons you teach to your son is how to seek out and surround himself with Christian friends.

You will face storms in your life: disappointment, pain, suffering, and temptation. Though these storms are common to all men, followers of Jesus Christ are called not to just deal with them, but also called to rejoice in them and stand firm in the power of His Word. To help you, God gave you His

Word and the Spirit of Christ, but God has also blessed you with the fellowship of other believers. From this fellowship with godly men you can surround yourself with support, guidance, and encouragement.

> **SURVIVAL NOTE**: Just as God will put good men in your lives at critical times to help guide and mentor you, Satan will use people to lead you astray. The difference is the people that Satan uses never know it—the perfect disguise.

What comes out of a man is what makes him unclean (Mark 7:20).

Location:

On your journey through this world you will face hardships, temptations, disappointment, and pain; these are the storms of life. Surrounding yourself with Christian friends and a church family acts like a ready-made shelter—the cave or overhang—you can turn to for guidance and support to help shield you from these storms. These preexisting relationships are the best forms of shelter. But what if you find yourself in unfamiliar territory or terrain? Maybe your family just moved to a new area, or your son is beginning a new school. In the wilderness there are places you should avoid building a shelter. Likewise, in the world there are people your son should be wary of.

But how does he identify those people? You must teach your son to observe. What are the people saying, and what words do they choose? How are they acting? Do they seek humor at the expense of others? Are they amused by things God detests? How a person behaves—publically and privately—speaks volumes about their character; and your son's ability to assess—not judge—an individual's character will hinge on his level of observation.

So what should he look for? Jesus said that we can recognize people by their fruit. The closer our son's personal relationship to Jesus is, the better his ability will be to recognize good fruit.

But the fruit of the Spirit is love, joy, peace, patience, kindness, goodness, faithfulness, gentleness and self-control (Galatians 5:22-23).

Galatians provides a good list of characteristics to look for in people.

SURVIVAL NOTE: Notice this list does not include personal interests, sense of humor, popularity, or wealth.

In the event your son is not aware of any Christian boys at school or in the neighborhood, you may have to search for "better ground" such as researching Christian youth programs or Christian men's fellowships at a local church for you. Asking friends and neighbors is another option. You will be amazed at what opportunities are available.

Therefore everyone who hears these words of mine and puts them into practice is like a wise man who built his house on the rock (Matthew 7:24).

Foundation:

Once you have identified someone who you think you want to be friends with, you need to determine if that person's beliefs are firmly founded in the Word of God. Is that person a believer? (Does he confess Jesus is the Son of God, born of a virgin, died on the cross paying the penalty for the sin of man, raised on the third day, sits at the right hand of the Father, and will return for His people and rule as King of Kings and Lord of Lords?) No doubt that is a big question for your son to ask someone they just met; maybe a good starting point is to teach your sons to ask, "Where do you go to church?"

SURVIVAL NOTE: Every time your son talks about a friend, teammate, or classmate ask your son where that person goes to church. If you ask your son often enough about his friends' beliefs, he will begin to ask his friends for himself. If that person does not attend church, have your son invite him to yours.

The Bible makes strong reference to building on a solid foundation. Having a strong foundation applies as much to survival shelters as fellowship. This is important because it is only upon a godly foundation that truly lasting and meaningful friendships can be built. These friendships are based on a shared faith in God and have a mutual trust rooted in understood expectations of thought and conduct.

Most of you know other Christian men, and your son most likely knows at least a few Christian kids. When you share your faith with others, make yourself available to them and demonstrate a consistent lifestyle that has evidence of a commitment to the Lord, others will be more inclined to enter into a relationship based on biblical values.

In him was life, and that life was the light of men (John 1:4).

Orientation:

Just as your shelter needs to be oriented toward the sun, you must ensure that the people you choose as friends or associates are oriented toward the Son. This constant focus on Jesus will cause you to be encouraged and uplifted even in the darkest and coldest of times of your life. These devoted followers of Christ will be the ones who will rejoice with you during the good times and stand firm with you in the bad. In a Christ-centered life, you will find fellowship that is based on trust, selflessness, and a desire to give. You can tell who your true friends are when times are bad.

SURVIVAL NOTE: If your life and relationships are oriented toward the Son—Jesus—even in the temporary absence of other believers you will never stand alone.

As iron sharpens iron, so one man sharpens another (Proverbs 27:17).

Resources:

Just like survival shelters, the resources you have available depend on two things: what you brought with you and the natural resources—based on your specific location—you have readily available. Inventory your resources. What did you bring with you? Do you possess the fruit of the Spirit? What preexisting (natural resources) opportunities are available for you and your son? Are you active in your church? Do you already have a circle of committed Christian friends?

The more resources you bring on your journey, the better prepared you will be to face the storms of life and just maybe avoid some of those storms altogether. Fathers must constantly strive to surround their sons with other Christian men and youth. Sunday school and Christian summer camps are a good place to start, but you must guide them farther.

Seek out and create opportunities for your son to interact with other Christian youth through various ministries or Christian based athletic organizations; encourage him to participate in your church youth organizations. Don't have anything like that? Start your own wilderness survival ministry! Become involved in the lives of your son's friends and create opportunities for your son to invite his friends to your house or to events that you organize.

Practice Your Survival Skills
Tent Camping
Time required: TBD
Equipment required:
• Bible
• Tent
• Ground mat
• Sleeping bag or blanket

Location:

Whether you choose your backyard, an improved camp-site at a park, or some place deep in the woods, be prepared to spend the night. Walk with your son and evaluate the different locations you may want to set up your tent. Discuss the pros and cons of each location.

Foundation:

Does the location you picked need to be cleared? Probably not, if you are in your backyard, but discuss how and why you use a stick to clear your shelter location.

Orientation:

Practice determining north using the stick and shadow method. Discuss the importance of orienting your shelter toward the sun.

Resources:

Resources? I brought a tent! Time yourselves and see how long it takes you to erect your tent.

Memory verse: Hebrews 10: 24-25
Discuss:
• How do your Christian friends and community help you in this world?
• How does surrounding yourself with a community of believers act like a tent in the wilderness?

Leaf Litter Shelter

Time required: one to three hours
Equipment required:

• Bible
• Axe or knife
• Old pair of underwear and an old shoe lace (The purpose for using underwear or shoelaces is to teach your son how to creatively think outside the box.)

Location:

Plan a hike in the woods with your son. On the hike identify and evaluate good locations to construct a shelter using only the above listed equipment.

Foundation:

Use a stick to clear leaf and debris from your shelter location. Determine if you need to dig a drainage trench around your shelter.

Orientation:

Practice determining north using the stick and shadow method (If you have a compass, check yourself for accuracy).

Resources:

Inventory your resources. Take a moment and discuss what equipment—other than the underwear and old shoelace—you brought with you that may be helpful in building a survival shelter. Do you have a jacket with a drawstring or a belt? Now take a moment and study the surrounding woods with your son. Discuss what possible building materials you observed on your walk to and at your chosen shelter location.

SURVIVAL NOTE: Remember, calories and sweat are valuable items in a survival situation; you do not want to waste them needlessly. First, identify and focus on items that can be used with the least amount of effort and modification.

Whether you decide to build a simple lean-to (for warmer climates) or a full leaf litter shelter, two simple rules apply: make your framework as sturdy as possible, and the thicker you pile on the leaves the less likely it will leak and the more insulation you will get. The rule of thumb for leaves is the thickness of your roof should be at least the length of your arm.

If you are modifying some natural feature or building the framework for your shelter from the ground up, ensure that your frame is sturdy enough to support weight. Once your framework is complete, begin working on your roof. Begin by laying pine or cedar boughs or sapling branches over the roof frame as this will help prevent leaves from falling into your shelter. Once this is done begin piling on leaves. After every twelve inches of leaves add additional pine or cedar boughs to hold them in place. Continue alternating like this until you have a roof as thick as your arm is long. Keep in mind that for leaf litter shelters, you must be sure to have adequate ventilation.

Once you have the roof and walls of your shelter built, you need to prepare the floor. First, lay pine boughs on the ground making a mat several inches thick. If possible, top the pine boughs with dry leaves or pine needles for added insulation and comfort. The more you have between you and the ground, the warmer you will be.

I recommend your floor to be at least six inches deep when compacted. Even if you have a sleeping bag or blanket, you will lose significant body heat to the ground unless you have something between you and the bare earth. Although not preferable, wet leaves can provide good insulation if they are thick enough.

SURVIVAL NOTE: A large trash bag is small enough to fit in the smallest of survival kits yet provides substantial insulation when filled with leaves.

Get in your shelter with your son.

Memory verse: Galatians 5:19-23

Discuss:

• Identify the fruit of the Spirit.
• What characteristics in people should we look for?
• What characteristics in people should we be wary of?

Snow Shelter

Time required: two to four hours

Equipment required:

• Bible
• Shovel or digging tool
•Lots of snow

Location:

Plan a winter hike or go into your backyard with your son. Identify and evaluate good locations to construct a snow shelter using the above listed equipment.

Foundation:

Examine your location and try to identify any potential hazards such as falling branches or avalanches.

Orientation:

In the winter, our two biggest concerns are cold and wind. If possible, orient your shelter walls perpendicular to prevailing winds.

Resources:

Those of you who grew up where it snows may have fond childhood memories of building snow forts or snow caves as you prepared for the impending neighborhood or schoolyard snowball fight. Building a snow shelter with your son will be just as much fun. Unlike snow forts designed to protect against the missiles of a pretend enemy, snow shelters are designed to protect against the extreme cold and wind. To do this adequately, you must build certain features into your shelter. Whether you are digging a snow cave out of a packed drift or building an Eskimo igloo or a snow trench, you must consider these basic design concepts:

- Make your shelter as snug as possible, only big enough for the number in your group.
- Make sure your sleeping area is higher than the top of your entrance hole.
- Make sure you have two ventilation holes—one low for air intake and one high for exhaust.
- Try to place something on your sleeping area between you and the snow. Pine or cedar boughs will work well and will keep the snow from melting under you and soaking your clothing.

SURVIVAL NOTE: Try to avoid sweating by working only as quickly as you must. If you get too sweaty, you'll be much colder when you lay down for the night.

Get in your shelter with your son.

Memory verse: Proverbs 13:20
Discuss:
- Why is a "companion of fools" destined to be hurt?
- How does spending time with wise people help you?

Make the Connection
Build Your Own Fellowship

Location:

Find and identify all the new opportunities for your son to create Christian fellowship opportunities—at his school, sports teams, or church youth groups for example. This may require doing some research. Ask other parents you know about various opportunities and events. Talk to your church leadership to learn what programs may be available.

Leadership Note: Make the program activities a priority with your schedule and resources. Get involved with the activities and encourage your son to participate.

You may decide to start your own Christian fellowship. Start by facilitating one activity. If the activity appears to meet the needs of others and generates support from your church leadership and other fathers, you may decide to make it a more formal and regular program. If you plan to start your own Christian fellowship, consider these basic principles:

Foundation:

The program content must be based on and consistent with the Word of God.

Orientation:

The goal of the program should be the discipleship of your son for the purpose of building godly character.

Resources:

Make a list of available resources. From this list you will decide on an activity.

Be creative. From fishing trips to all-night video game competitions, the interests of the boys will play a part in choosing the activity. But don't be afraid to challenge them to try new activities. Once you have chosen an activity based on the resources available, it's time to start planning. Like everything we do, the first step is to take it to the Lord in prayer. The second step is to discuss it with your church leadership for support and guidance. You should also solicit the advice of other fathers.

- Develop a written mission statement.
- Identify an activity, its location, the date that the activity will occur, and identify the resources that will be required.
- Assign tasks to everyone that will be participating in the activity.
- Supervise and evaluate the activity. Don't be shy about asking for feedback or constructive criticism.
- Have fun with your son

You have been a refuge for the poor, a refuge for the needy in his distress, a shelter from the storm and a shade from the heat. For the breath of the ruthless is like a storm driving against a wall and like the heat of the desert (Isaiah 25:4).

As a father you are the head coach. The good thing about being head coach is that you get to decide who makes the team. By creating wholesome situations and quality relationships for your son—surrounding him with godly men—you are helping to pick his teammates for his journey through this world. The fellowship you must encourage above all else is fellowship with Jesus; only through your son's personal relationship with God will he will find the true refuge, strength, and courage he needs to endure the storms of life as well as receive lasting peace and eternal salvation.

Chapter 7

A Father's Blessing

This is my Son, whom I love; with him I am well pleased (Matthew 3:17).

At the heart of all sound teaching through the centuries, whether within military institutions or without, has dwelt the simple idea that every vigorous man needs some kind of contest, some realization of resistance overcome, before he can feel that he is making the best use of his faculties.[6] —Col. S.L.A. Marshall

Fourteen years of training, six months of planning, revising, "what-ifing," and it all came down to a day that will forever be etched into my heart and mind: the day my son became a man.

The thermometer in our kitchen window read twenty-one degrees Fahrenheit when my oldest son Jake and I left the house about 8:30 on that Saturday morning. As we drove the three miles to a trailhead parking area in an adjacent National forest, I tried to keep the conversation light. After all, we were only going for a walk. Avoiding his eyes, I shouldered the fifty pound pack I had carefully prepared, and I grabbed the walking stick. I knew they would raise questions, and my mind was racing. *Did I remember everything? Was everyone in place? Was he really ready for this?* Still, I managed to conceal my anxiety enough simply to say, "Follow me" and led him down the trail.

"You know, this trail is like your life," I began. "You have never been on it, so you really don't know what is around the next bend; but as a man, you must be prepared to deal with whatever you encounter. It is also like your life because now we are together. In fact, I am leading the way for you."

I saw a grapefruit sized stone alongside the trail; it would do nicely. It was time. I stopped and turned to face him. *God, give me wisdom and strength.*

"But very soon, you will leave our home; or maybe I'll be gone, and you will have to be the man of the house. Then you will have to walk alone. Son, there is something I want you to do for yourself and for me. The rest of this journey you must face alone. Everything I possess, even my very life, I give to you freely, if you choose to accept it." I pulled the pack off my back and held it out to him. A curious expression came over his face as he took the pack and hefted it onto his back. Jake said nothing but simply stared at me with a mildly perplexed expression.

I returned my gaze to the stone, which seemed to weigh at least fifteen pounds. After three firm kicks, it broke free from the frozen soil. "One thing you must also do on this journey," I reached down, picked up the frozen stone and placed it in Jake's bare hands, "you must carry this with you." He looked into his hand, felt the heft of the stone and the bite of the cold into his flesh, and then looked back at me. His expression never changed.

"This trail represents your life. Stay on the path and do not turn to the left or the right." I placed a whistle around his neck and then paraphrased 1 Kings 2:2, "Your journey is ahead of you. When you see my face again your journey is done." I could barely keep my voice from cracking. My mouth was dry. He continued to look at me, unflinching.

Even as I write this, I remain humbled and amazed that Jake never asked me a single question. In fact, he never said a word; it was as if were thinking, *Dad, whatever your putting me up against, I trust you.* The time had come for us to part.

"May God bless you," I said as I hugged him, my voice not even sounding as if it were my own. Then he turned and stepped off down the trail. Within thirty seconds Jake had vanished into the wilderness and a flood of emotion swept me: joy, fear, and doubt. *Is he ready?* I fell to my knees and prayed hard for Jake's journey—so hard in fact, that I felt all the angels in heaven heard me. They must have, because God blessed the next twenty-four hours in ways I did not imagine possible.

The rules were simple: six men chosen by me, either in person or through letters would define, from their perspective, what God expects from a man. I offered no input or advice to these men. Additionally, no one could tell Jake what would happen on the journey. "All things shall be revealed" was the only information he could receive about the events unfolding. In addition to their collective wisdom, each man was to share his favorite verse from the Bible and why.

Jake encountered Wayne after he had gone a mile and a half. Wayne sat beside a tree twenty feet off the trail to Jake's right. As Jake drew opposite Wayne's position, he stopped and leaned forward at the waist to relieve the biting shoulder straps and the weight of the pack. His eyes were focused on the ground at his feet so he did not notice Wayne until he heard his name called.

Surprised, Jake recovered quickly and immediately relaxed upon seeing a familiar face. Wayne is a close friend of mine. Wayne approached Jake and began his first formal lesson of what would be a very long journey. First, Wayne shared with Jake the importance of being observant of one's environment and making an effort to interpret what is seen—and even what is not seen but should be.

Wayne allowed that to sink in a moment before moving on to his pack. Wayne asked Jake what was in his pack. "I don't know," he replied, "but it weighs a ton." Wayne had him remove the pack and set it on the ground between them. "Before you go further on your journey, you have to know what you already have. In other words, take careful inventory of your resources," Wayne instructed. "A man has to know what tools or instruments he has available to him in order to make decisions. It helps him know what his options are in any situation," he added. He had Jake take everything out of the pack and place it on the trail, asking him what each item was for as he set it aside.

After a thorough inventory of the rucksack, Wayne asked him what he learned from the process. "I guess I have the resources to stay out here for a while," he replied.

"Very true; you have a lot of options with this kit," Wayne responded. "Just be sure to make use of them when the need arises." After repacking the rucksack, Wayne had Jake sit down on a log and told him about how he and I had met back in our first of four long years at the Virginia Military Institute. He related some of our early experiences together and how and why our friendship had begun and been sustained.

Wayne's purpose, as he later shared with me, was to make Jake aware of what kind of friend I was to him early on during a particularly difficult first year at VMI. He wanted Jake to learn something about his dad that would make him proud—but more importantly—show him how an early encounter set the tone for a lifelong friendship. He also wanted Jake to understand how God puts other men in our lives at challenging times for reasons we don't fully comprehend at the time.

"At the end of the day," Wayne concluded, "regardless of the circumstances we find ourselves in, we must be humble in our dealings with those God puts in our paths and treat them with kindness and dignity." They then returned to the trail, and Wayne walked with Jake for a quarter mile before stopping at the top of a gentle rise where the trail turned sharply to the right to follow the contour line of the steep ridge they were descending.

From here, the woods opened up enough for the trail ahead to be clearly visible for several hundred yards. "Jake," he said, "you have to continue from here alone. Stay on the path and keep moving. God will be with you." With a hesitant goodbye, Jake turned and began moving down the trail again.

A mile and a half further, Shawn was waiting for Jake. Shawn revealed the meaning of the pack and the stone. The pack, he explained, was his load to bear. Just as his Father in heaven has equipped him with everything he needs to survive his journey in life, his father equipped him with everything he needed to survive this journey. "A man carries his own load," Shawn told Jake, "even if it feels heavy at times. God never gives us more than we can handle."

The stone represented sin. Once Jake knew what it represented, he had the opportunity to lay it at the foot of the cross. Jake happily cast the stone away and tried to ease the pain in his frozen, aching fingers. It was a lesson Jake will never forget because it was forged during three painful miles on a rugged mountain trail.

Shawn also gave my son a prayer journal to document his adventure and what he had learned. In the prayer journal were three letters: one from his grandfather, one from his uncle, and one from me. The letter took me a month to write; it was my "death bed" advice to Jake.

Shawn then led Jake off the trail and into a remote, densely wooded draw. Shawn explained that he had to wait there. Shawn was not allowed to tell Jake what to do but could prompt him with survival questions. Slowly, a camp took shape. At a distance, I began to smell smoke. I was pleased; Jake had no matches.

Once the camp was prepared, Shawn sat with Jake and took him on a scriptural journey to reveal the Seven Points of Valor: honor, courage, chivalry, purity, loyalty, obedience, and dedication.

At 2:00 p.m., Shawn told my son it was time for him to go. Jake asked Shawn how long he would be there. Shawn told him, "All things shall be revealed. Wait here, when you see your father's face again, your journey is done."

By 7:15 on Sunday morning, the temperature was still only nineteen degrees. I had to guide Roy into the forest and show him where Jake was; I stayed back. Roy found Jake curled around his fire trying to stay warm. About an hour later, when it was clear that Roy had finished his lesson, I walked into the camp. All I could see was Jake's beaming smile as I came closer; he had seen his father's face again, and his journey was done!

Tears welled in my eyes as I hugged him. I then looked Jake squarely in the eyes and shook his hand. "There is little else anyone can tell you about what God expects from a man. But how you choose to apply these lessons to your everyday life will determine what sort of man you will become." We all shared communion at the camp—a moving experience that brought a sense of deep peace and satisfaction as a father such as I had never known before.

To commemorate his accomplishment, I presented Jake with a gift—a survival knife—a man's knife he had clearly earned. As we helped Jake break camp, I offered to carry his pack out for him. I knew his body ached from the exertions of the past twenty-four hours; he had hardly eaten, had almost no sleep, and had no idea how far we had to go. He looked at me with a smile and said, "That's all right, Dad; I'll carry my own load." And he did.

"Did you think you would be spending the night out here when we left home yesterday?" I asked. Jake smiled, shook his head, and said, "I didn't think Mom would allow it!" I smiled inwardly at his reasoning.

"What was going through your mind when it got dark, and you realized no one was coming for you?" He looked at me, paused for a few seconds, searching for a way to express what had clearly been a challenging event, and said, "At first, I was really upset. Then I opened my Bible and read the twenty-third Psalm, and that calmed me down a lot. Then I reread the letters people wrote for me, and that made me feel good knowing how much people really cared about me."

Jake then told me that when his fire went out, he realized how easy it was to depend more on a fire for security and comfort than on God. "Without the fire, it got cold, dark, and pretty scary; and I began to pray. Though I was able to make another fire, I knew that real peace and comfort can only come when we rely on God."

As I led Jake out of the wilderness I asked, "On a scale of one to ten, how was it?"

Jake's face grew a big smile. "It was a twenty! It was awesome, Dad."

In the hours of loneliness, in the cold and dark stillness of the forest, Jake and I both waged war against giants. Jake struggled against the panic that comes from fear, frustration, confusion, and isolation. I battled against the doubts that clouded my mind—doubt in myself, my judgment, and why I shouldn't rush to my son's side to reassure and protect him.

In both cases, we turned to prayer and the Word for strength and assurance. Jake and I won our battles; we defeated our Goliath with the only weapon that could work in such circumstances—our faith in God, our ultimate Father. And through it all, we were both reminded in a gentle and uplifting way that we are never alone; our Father, who is in heaven, is also right here with us.

Fourteen years ago I had witnessed the birth of my son and named him. When he was twelve, I baptized him in a river. On a cold December morning, I gave Jake my blessing and named him a man. In my letter to Jake, I left nothing unsaid. I am at peace. My son received a gift—the gift of godly wisdom. I could not have given him this treasure in a thousand lifetimes; it was not mine to give. The wisdom came from men far greater than I—men I admire who were willing to pour out their collective wisdom into a young man deep in the wilderness. I am forever in their debt.

I led a fourteen-year-old boy into the wilderness and then sent him forward alone. Twenty-four hours later I walked out with a man. I have two more sons to go. God is great.

He who overcomes will inherit all this, and I will be his God and he will be my son (Revelation 21:7).

Jake was uniquely qualified for this journey for two reasons: Jake had grown up exploring the woods and had also been an active participant in our wilderness survival ministry for over two years. The journey was intended to challenge my son and take him out of his comfort zone—not break him—so that God, the message, and the men would have my son's undivided attention.

Jake had been trained with the skills and knowledge he needed to survive a frigid December night deep in the wilderness. As I look back on the journey, anything less would have cheated him out of reaching his full potential. Now, as I look forward to this experience with my other two sons, I know that each will earn his passage into Christian manhood with journeys very different from Jake's—each according to his own needs.

The Lord bless you and keep you; the Lord make his face shine upon you and be gracious to you; the Lord turn his face toward you and give you peace (Numbers 6:24-26).

The importance of a father's blessing cannot be over-stated. According to *Webster's New Ideal Dictionary*, a blessing is "to invoke divine care or protection for; to praise, glorify; to confer prosperity or happiness upon."[7] God knew the power and importance of a father's blessing, and the blessing on the banks of the Jordan River helped Jesus stand firm against the devil himself. And just as Jesus, the only Son of the living God, needed his Father's blessing, so too does your son need your blessing. It is our son's quest for this blessing that drives him to achieve and will echo deep in his heart when times are tough, remaining there long after you are gone.

One thing to keep in mind as you begin the quest to train your son to be a godly man, prepared not just to survive in this wilderness that is life in the twenty-first century, but also to bring honor and glory to the King, you must give your blessing when it is earned in accordance with God's will. A father's blessing is also our inheritance—the "ripple" that we leave behind. What will be the legacy of your ripple? Cars, property, and trust funds are nice if you have them to give, but nothing on this earth that you can give your son will give him the kind of peace and assurance that penetrates both the mind and soul. This only comes by way of faith to those who fear God and have found their redemption in Christ Jesus.

I will make your name great, and you will be a blessing (Genesis 12:2).

So, what's in a name? In all likelihood, you chose your son's name. But a name is often meaningless unless you also give your son his identity as a Christian man. Identity is more than what we are called; it is who we are. Through your son's understanding of his identity as a Christian man, he will discover his purpose in God's kingdom. Your responsibility is to train, lead, and direct your son and provide a consistent biblical example for him. This training will cause your son to begin to discover his identity. It is never too early to begin training your son.

Beginning Early

On a cold, rainy April day, deep in the Shenandoah Mountains, five-year-old Cole stood silently, surrounded by his father and several other men and boys, before a campfire holding his blanket. It was a special day, Cole's fifth birthday, and it was not just any blanket, it was *his* blanket—the strongest symbol that bound him to his infancy. "You are no longer Momma's baby boy," Shawn said. "You are now Papa's big boy." With these words, Cole dropped his blanket into the fire. Cole stood silently, watching as the blanket ignited, reflecting on his new role as a young man in his father's house.

There were new rules, new expectations, and new privileges. Cole knew what was expected of him and was excited. Shawn had spent weeks instructing and preparing Cole for this very day. On that rainy April day, Cole received a blessing from his father—far more than just a name, "Papa's big boy." He was given the blessing of a new identity and role in his father's house.

Similarly, encourage the young men to be self-controlled. In everything set them an example by doing what is good. In your teaching show integrity, seriousness and soundness of speech that cannot be condemned, so that those who op-

pose you may be ashamed because they have nothing bad to say about us (Titus 2:6-8).

Be a living example of godly manhood. This is the beginning of all training and sets the stage for everything to follow. No words or single deed can ever match a godly life lived; and it will be your example, the unspoken life lessons, that will cause the greatest ripple to shape and direct your son more than anything else. The living example that you set establishes your credibility, opens lines of honest communication, and helps to lay the foundation for your son's trust and confidence in you as a leader, teacher, and mentor.

To lead by example means you have to be there—physically present and mentally engaged—as an active and willing participant in his daily activities, teaching him how to respond in good times and bad, through victory and defeat. Living out your life as an example also means showing him, through your actions and words, how you deal with the conflict, people, and events encountered in life.

. . . strengthening the disciples and encouraging them to remain true to the faith. "We must go through many hardships to enter the kingdom of God (Acts 14:22).

Affirm your son's identity as a follower of Christ and encourage him to grow in faith, love, and knowledge of His ways. This means encouraging your son to read God's Word, to teach the importance of prayer, of Christian service, and of fellowship. At some point in your son's life, you will not be there to tell him right from wrong or shield him from all the dead ends that this world makes so appealing. Will he be alone or walk confidently with Jesus? Much easier said than done, I know. Although bad things can happen to good people, how you respond to the challenges and setbacks that you face will teach your son more about dealing with the harsh realities of life than any amount of platitudes.

Young men must understand that even the godliest of men will at some point encounter the sharp corners and rough edges of life in a way that tests their faith. Remember the lessons of Job and the basis for the trials that God allowed Satan to inflict on him. Will a godly man's faith endure under severe strain? We must affirm the fact that our sons were created to be men and that God has a plan for each of their lives.

> *Brothers, I do not consider myself yet to have taken hold of it. But one thing I do: Forgetting what is behind and straining toward what is ahead, I press on toward the goal to win the prize for which God has called me heavenward in Christ Jesus* (Philippians 3:13-14).

Jake's journey toward godly manhood is by no means complete; none of our journeys are until we see our Father's face. In four short years my eldest son will leave my house and venture forth to take his place as a man in this world. Two more sons and a daughter will follow him. The reality is they will be under my stewardship for a brief time until they begin making decisions and choices on their own. Only God knows the ripple I have created; only He knows what legacy I will leave behind. Four short years . . . until then I will continue to lead, guide, and mentor, praying for my children continually.

But if serving the Lord seems undesirable to you, then choose for yourselves this day whom you will serve . . . But as for me and my household, we will serve the Lord (Joshua 24:15).

Suggested Wilderness Survival Kit

What goes into your personal survival kit will depend largely on where you live and your personal preference. Most people have some idea of what items they feel are indispensable and should modify their kit accordingly. The following are some items that we recommend should be in every kit.

Bible
BlastMatch ™ (magnesium and flint fire starting device)
WetFire ™ (fire starting tinder)
Para (550) Cord – at least 50'
Fishing hooks (various sizes)
Knife (fixed blade or lock blade folding knife)
Water purification tablets
Metal cup
Canteen
2 Plastic trash bags
4' x 6' sheet of clear plastic
Poncho
First aid kit
Leather work gloves

BIBLIOGRAPHY

1 Hefling, Kimberly, "Army recruiters laying out 'buffet' of signing benefits," Associated Press; Appeared in the August 10, 2007 edition of the Northern Virginia Daily.

2 Marshall, S.L.A (Col. USA); *A Soldiers Load and the Mobility of a Nation Quantico*, VA: Marine Corps Association. June, 1980, 47-48.

3 United States Air Force, *Search and Rescue SURVIVAL AFM 64-5*; Washington, DC, U.S. Government Printing Office, 1969, 2-46.

4 United States Air Force, *AFM 64-5*. 2-47.

5 Hendricks, Howard G. & Hendricks, William D: *Living by the Book.* Moody, 2007.

6 Marshall; *A Soldiers Load and the Mobility of a Nation.*

7 *Webster's New Ideal Dictionary*, G. & C. Merriam Co., 1973.

About the Authors

Todd Freiwald grew up in New Mexico where he spent his time camping, hunting, fishing, and exploring Indian caves. He graduated from the Virginia Military Institute in 1988 and went on to serve in the United States Marine Corps. Upon leaving the Marines he was appointed as a special agent in the United States Secret Service. After leaving the Secret Service he became a special agent in the Department of Justice where he currently focuses on violent crime, gangs, and drug trafficking. Todd and Wendy have been married for twenty years and have four children: Jake, Ryan, Scott, and Megan. He is an active member of his church and coordinates the Father/ Son Wilderness Survival Ministry in Woodstock, Virginia.

Shawn McQuaid and his wife, Laura have been married for over 16 years and have two children, Cole and Erin. Shawn received a one year Bible certificate from Montana Wilderness School of the Bible and graduated from the Alaska Bible College. Shawn teaches Bible study methods and other adult learning classes at his church. Shawn is currently an investigator at a regional jail, was the facilities tactical team commander for over ten years, and maintains the position of general instructor and firearms instructor.

To contact them with questions or to arrange speaking engagements, please email: tfwilderness@gmail.com